More advance acclaim for
The Power of Nice

"In a dog-eat-dog world where so many seem prepared to do whatever it takes to get ahead, Linda Kaplan Thaler and Robin Koval point out that it is truly the quiet, kind gesture that speaks most loudly. 'Please,' 'Thank You,' and 'No, You First' really are key words that should be a part of every go-getter's lexicon. *The Power of Nice* should become the new bible for those looking to hit the top."

—Deborah Norville, host of *Inside Edition*, the longest-running newsmagazine

"Having matured during the most savage era of entertainment, I can vouch for the fact that being nice is one sure means of success. Nice guys do finish on top."

—Dick Clark

"If the Power of Nice equates to: caring for other people, having honor, working with honesty, competing with dignity, sharing knowledge, and behaving with kindness, then 'The Power of Nice' should be a mandatory business seminar at every major university. Can you imagine if Enron executives had practiced the Power of Nice?"

—Marcia Gay Harden

"Though a lively . . . read, this is not a cutesy little bon-bon of a book. Well thought-out and crisply presented, it offers key principles, case studies, and exercises to help make niceness habitual."

—*Publishers Weekly*

Dear Charlotte -

You're living proof nice works. Thanks for all your support.

Linda Kaplan Thaler
Robin Koval

The Power of Nice

How to Conquer the Business World with Kindness

Linda Kaplan Thaler and Robin Koval

Foreword by Jay Leno

NEW YORK · LONDON · TORONTO · SYDNEY · AUCKLAND

A CURRENCY BOOK
PUBLISHED BY DOUBLEDAY

This book is not to be confused with the previously published **The Power of Nice: How to Negotiate So Everyone Wins, Especially You!**, by Ronald M. Shapiro and Mark Jankowski. And see www.Shapironegotiations.com.

Published in the United States by Doubleday, an imprint of The Doubleday Broadway Publishing Group, a division of Random House, Inc., New York.
www.currencybooks.com

Book design by Diane Hobbing

Cataloging-in-Publication Data is on file with the Library of Congress.

ISBN-13: 978-0-385-51892-5
ISBN-10: 0-385-51892-7

PRINTED IN THE UNITED STATES OF AMERICA

SPECIAL SALES
Currency Books are available at special discounts for bulk purchases for sales promotions or premiums. Special editions, including personalized covers, excerpts of existing books, and corporate imprints, can be created in large quantities for special needs. For more information, write to Special Markets, Currency Books, specialmarkets@randomhouse.com.

10 9 8 7 6 5 4 3 2 1

First Edition

To my parents, Bertha and Marvin,
for teaching me the value of kindness.

—Linda Kaplan Thaler

To my sister, Joyce, a woman born with
the power of nice in her heart.

—Robin Koval

Acknowledgments

First, a heartfelt thank-you to Tricia Kenney, Managing Director of Corporate Communications at The Kaplan Thaler Group, for giving us the perfect title for this book. How fitting for Tricia to have made such a critical contribution, because she is, in fact, one of the nicest (not to mention one of the smartest) people we know. Tricia, your passion and dedication to making *The Power of Nice* a reality was truly remarkable.

Thanks to Richard Abate, our brilliant literary agent at ICM. You have amazing insight and impeccable taste, and can always be counted on to be our staunchest advocate.

Words alone cannot express the depth of our thanks to Sara Eckel, an amazing and talented writer, without whom this book would still be a dream in our hearts. Sara was always able to find the insightful quote, the illuminating story, and the imaginative phrase that would perfectly weave all our thoughts and experiences together. A very special thank-you to Mark Holcomb, for always being there for Sara.

A special thanks to our talented and dedicated editor, Roger Scholl at Doubleday. Roger, your additions (and deletions) always have the perfect touch. Every page in *The Power of Nice* has benefited from your talent and passion for this project. We would also like to thank the entire team at

Doubleday for your support of *The Power of Nice*—especially Rex Bonomelli, who created the perfect book cover, Meredith McGinnis, Michael Palgon, and Laura Pillar. Our thanks also go to the folks at Dan Klores Communications—Karyn Barr, Johanna Flattery, Wendy Katz, and Jeff Klein, our tireless publicists, who have used their wonderful skills to help us bring *The Power of Nice* to the public. To Toby Fleishman, who masterfully managed the book marketing process from start to finish, thank you for keeping us on track every step of the way. Thanks to our generous friends Evan Greenberg and Diane Bell at Allscope Media for giving so much of their time and media savvy. Thanks also to Mike Metz and the talented team at Fat Free Studio for designing our wonderful website and to Joanna Parson for her superfast transcriptions.

A heartfelt thanks to Gerry Laybourne, who so generously gave us an opportunity to speak about the power of nice at the Oxygen Mentors Walk breakfast, a national event which she created in 2005. And thank you as well to Amy Gross, Editor-in-Chief at *O, The Oprah Magazine,* for being in the audience that morning and recognizing that this idea could become an article for the magazine. These are the events that ultimately prompted us to write our book, and we thank you both for recognizing the full potential of this idea.

We especially want to thank the many clients, friends, relatives, and coworkers who have so generously contributed their stories or helped find them for this book: Susan Arnold, Elizabeth Cogwell Baskin, Gordon Bethune, Marialisa Calta, Richard Davis, Bob Eckel, Howard Eckel,

Frank Finney, Bonnie French, Hal Friedman, Robbie Finke, Claire Geier, Marla Ginsburg, Jonathan Gordon, Lynn Harris, Tony Hassini, Diane Karnett, Jennifer Voight Kaplan, Ruth Downing Karp, Jill Kirschenbaum, A. G. Lafley, Shira Miller, Joanne Miserandino, Charlotte Otto, Erin Peck, Rachel Eve Pine, Whitney Anne Postman, Ph.D., Gail Richards, John Robinson, Helene Stapinski, Sheldon Smith, Jennifer Stoner, and Lupe Valdez.

A very special thank-you to Maurice Lévy, the CEO of our parent company, Publicis Groupe. Your enthusiastic support for this endeavor is truly appreciated. Thanks to Eve Magnant, for all your fact-checking efforts.

Through the many months of working on this, many people at The Kaplan Thaler Group have helped with their advice, overtime hours, and support. Special thanks to our tireless assistants, Sheryl Genna and Fran Marzano, for always being there when we need them. Thank you to the members of our Executive Committee—Lisa Bifulco, Tricia Kenney, Gerry Killeen, and Kevin Sweeney—each of whom has helped with the demands of making this book a reality. Thanks to Dennis Marchesiello and the KTG Studio for helping to create the original book proposal. Thanks to John Vila for helping to proofread the acknowledgments and manuscript. Thanks also to Peter Unger and John Colquhoun for your wonderful cover designs and fabulous illustrations for our initial proposal. Additional thanks to Myles Kleeger for his work on the marketing programs for *The Power of Nice,* as well as to the tireless efforts of Erin Creagh for all details large and small.

A special thank-you to the experts who gave us much

needed input into the underlying human truth behind *The Power of Nice,* Dr. Ona Robinson and Dr. Gary Belkin.

Sincere thanks to the brilliant Geshe Michael Roach, who inspired the beginnings of this book with his simple, insightful remark that we should all bake a bigger pie.

A grateful note of thanks to Donald Trump, for his gracious support; Ken Auletta, for his honesty and wisdom; and Kathy Ireland, for her kind words and inspiration.

And of course our heartfelt thanks to our respective families:

To my wonderful husband, Fred Thaler, for all your loving support, and to our children, Michael and Emily, who are a constant source of joy and happiness.

To my beloved husband, Kenny Koval, whose unfailing faith in me is always a source of inspiration. And to my beautiful and talented daughter, Melissa Koval: You fill my life with joy and pride.

And finally, our deepest thanks to Jay Leno, for showing us the true power of nice by sharing his wonderful stories and graciously contributing the Foreword to this book.

To everyone we have included here on these pages, and to the many people who have touched our lives and made us nicer for it, we hope this book helps you enjoy your successes and brings you the happiness you seek.

—Linda and Robin

Contents

Foreword by Jay Leno xiii

Chapter 1: The Power of Nice 1

Chapter 2: The Six Power of Nice Principles 6

Chapter 3: Bake a Bigger Pie 16

Chapter 4: Sweeten the Deal 29

Chapter 5: Help Your Enemies 41

Chapter 6: Tell the Truth 57

Chapter 7: "Yes" Your Way to the Top 76

Chapter 8: Shut Up and Listen 90

Chapter 9: Put Your Head on Their Shoulders 100

Chapter 10: Create a Nicer Universe 116

Notes 121

Index 123

Foreword

BY JAY LENO

To me, one of the greatest books ever written is Charles Dickens's *A Christmas Carol.* Why? Because of its simple premise: Doing the right thing makes you feel better. It's not a religious thing. It's just that doing good things will improve your life. Let's face it, you cannot eat the whole pie or you'll make yourself sick. Eat some, and then give whatever is left over to other people.

When I was asked to be interviewed for *The Power of Nice,* I said yes not just because I wanted to be nice. I did so because I think it's the right way to be. But today being nice is so surprising it becomes a news story. I recently told a joke on the show and got a letter from a woman saying she was offended by it. I called her to apologize and say that I was sorry if I hurt her feelings. For some reason, she contacted the newspapers, and my apology became headline news! We live in a society where common courtesy is so *uncommon* that it is treated as though you just saved someone's life by giving them the Heimlich maneuver.

Even if you get into an auto accident, insurance companies will tell you not to apologize. It's an admission of guilt. So what do they want you to do? Run away and call your attorney? Yet, my guess is that if it's your fault and you do apologize, nine times out of ten people will be grateful and probably nicer back about getting the damage repaired. So many of today's problems can be solved with simple acts of kindness.

Being nice is especially important when you have a platform like *The Tonight Show.* It can't be a bully pulpit or an ego booster. There's a reason the show is called *The Tonight Show with Jay Leno* instead of *The Tonight Show Starring Jay Leno.* It's because of my mother. She thought saying, "Starring Jay Leno" would tell audiences, "Oh, look at me, I'm a Big Shot." So I said to her, "Okay, Ma. How about 'with Jay Leno'?"

Life is not that hard. Try giving a little. You would be surprised at how much you get back.

The Power of Nice

Chapter 1

The Power of Nice

For years, we have loved a particular security guard in our Manhattan office building. In fact, most of us at The Kaplan Thaler Group think the world of him. A large, jovial man in his mid-fifties, Frank brightens people's days by giving everyone who walks into our building a huge, warm greeting. "Hello, Linda!" "Hello, Robin!" he'll say. "Happy Friday!"

Frank's engaging banter changed the way we started work in the morning. Instead of simply flashing our passes anonymously and making a beeline for the elevator, we found ourselves seeking out Frank and making sure to say hello. He set a positive tone for the entire day. But we never considered how Frank might be helping our business, other than preventing intruders from entering the premises.

That is, until the day Richard Davis, the president and COO of U.S. Bank, the sixth-largest bank in the United States, came to see us. For months, our entire team at The Kaplan Thaler Group had been working to create a pitch that would wow Davis and win us the huge U.S. Bank account.

At the time of Davis's visit, it was down to the wire. We were one of two agencies still in the running for the account. Davis and his team were flying in from their executive offices in Minneapolis to meet personally with us. We didn't realize it at the time, but in fact Davis and his staff were a bit apprehensive about the kind of treatment they'd get in New York City. The furious pace and hard-bitten "out of my way" attitude of the Big Apple had become part of the mythology of the city. They were afraid we would be too cold, too aloof.

But when Richard Davis and his team walked into our building, they received a warm, enthusiastic greeting from Frank. When Davis reached our offices a few minutes later, he was gushing about the friendly security guard. "This guy gave me a huge hello!" he said. "And all of a sudden, I thought how could I *not* want to work with a company that has someone like Frank? How can I feel anything but good about hiring an agency like that?" We won the account.

Of course, Davis wouldn't have awarded us the job if he wasn't impressed with our work. But we've gotta give Frank credit. With a multimillion-dollar account in the balance, it was Frank's warm hello that helped us cinch the deal.

That is the power of nice.

The security guard wins the heart of the COO. It might sound like a Disney movie, but we can assure you it was no fantasy. We wrote *The Power of Nice* because we completely disagreed with the conventional wisdom that "Nice guys finish last" and "No good deed goes unpunished." Our culture has helped to propagate the myth of social Darwinism—of survival of the fittest—that the cutthroat "me vs. you" philosophy wins the day. One of the biggest-selling career books in the past few years is called *Nice Girls Don't Get the Corner Office.* Yet this completely contradicts the way we have run our business and our lives. In less than a decade, we built The Kaplan Thaler Group into a powerhouse in advertising with close to $1 billion in billings, making it one of the nation's fastest-growing advertising agencies. Our success was won not with pitchforks and spears, but with flowers and chocolates. Our growth is the result not of fear and intimidation, but of smiles and compliments.

Time and time again, we have seen the extraordinary power of nice in our business dealings and in our personal lives. It is the patient passenger who politely asks the airline ticket agent to please check one more time who gets the first-class upgrade, rather than the "I'm a triple platinum member" blowhard. It is the driver who is polite and apologetic to the police officer who sometimes is forgiven for driving over the speed limit.

But nice has an image problem. Nice gets no respect. To be labeled "nice" usually means the other person has little else positive to say about you. To be nice is to be considered Pollyanna and passive, wimpy, and Milquetoast. Let us be clear: *Nice is not naïve.* Nice does not mean smiling blandly while others walk all over you. Nice does not mean being a doormat. In fact, we would argue that *nice is the toughest four-letter word you'll ever hear.* It means moving forward with the clear-eyed confidence that comes from knowing that being very nice and placing other people's needs on the same level as your own will get you everything you want. Think about it:

- *Nice is luckier in love.* People who are low-key and congenial have one-half the divorce rate of the general population, says a University of Toronto study.[1]

- *Nice makes more money.* According to Professor Daniel Goleman, who conducted research on how emotions affect the workplace for his book *Primal Leadership,* there is a direct correlation between employee morale and the bottom line. One study found that every 2 percent increase in the service climate—that is, the general cheerfulness and helpfulness of the staff—saw a 1 percent increase in revenue.[2]

- *Nice is healthier.* A University of Michigan study found that older Americans who provide support to others—either through volunteer work or simply by being a good friend and neighbor—had a 60 percent lower rate of premature death than their unhelpful peers.

- *Nice spends less time in court.* One study found that doctors who had never been sued spoke to their patients for an average of three minutes longer than physicians who had been sued twice or more, reports Malcolm Gladwell in his book *Blink: The Power of Thinking Without Thinking.*

It is often the small kindnesses—the smiles, gestures, compliments, favors—that make our day and can even change our lives. Whether you are leading your own company, running for president of the PTA, or just trying to conduct a civil conversation with your teenage daughter, the power of nice will help you break through the misconceptions that keep you from achieving your goals. The power of nice will help you to open doors, improve your relationships at work and at home, and let you sleep a whole lot better. Nice not only finishes first; those who use its nurturing power wind up happier, to boot!

In the chapters ahead, we'll show you that being nice doesn't mean sacrificing what you want for someone else. There's always a second, third, or even fourth solution when you apply the principles of nice.

Chapter 2

The Six Power of Nice Principles

The Power of Nice Principle #1

Positive impressions are like seeds.

Every time you smile at a messenger, laugh at a coworker's joke, thank an assistant, or treat a stranger with graciousness and respect, you throw off positive energy. That energy makes an impression on the other person that, in turn, is passed along to and imprinted on the myriad others he or she meets. Such imprints have a multiplier effect. And ultimately, those favorable impressions find their way back to you. That doesn't mean the waiter you tipped well will one day found a Fortune 100 company and offer you stock options (unless it was one hell of a tip). The results of the power of nice are rarely that direct. In fact, you may not notice any impact on your life for years, apart from the warm glow it gives you inside. Nonetheless, we have found that the power of nice has a domino effect. You may not ever be able to trace your good fortune back to a specific encounter, but it is a mathematical certainty that the power of nice lays the groundwork for many opportunities down the road. These positive impressions are like seeds. You plant them and forget about them, but underneath the surface, they're growing and expanding, often exponentially.

Here's an example of how the power of nice has worked for us. Not long ago, we featured Donald Trump's wife, Melania, in an Aflac commercial, at the suggestion of Aflac chairman and CEO Daniel Amos. We gave Mrs. Trump, as one of the stars of the commercial, her own trailer and made sure she was comfortable and had everything she needed. Our team treated her nicely not because she was married to a famous person, but because we have a policy of being polite and respectful to all the talent on our advertising shoots.

Months later, the producers of *The Apprentice* asked Linda to be a judge on one of the shows, in which the apprentice hopefuls were required to create a car advertisement:

Before the first segment was shot, I introduced myself to Donald Trump, mentioning that we were the agency that had used his wife in an Aflac duck commercial. Well, Trump clearly remembered his wife's experience, because right before the shooting started, he leaned over and said, "You were so nice to my wife. Watch how I return the favor."

Then he got on and described The Kaplan Thaler Group as one of the hottest ad agencies in the country—on network television! He then went out of his way to include me in the on-camera discussions. All because we were nice to his wife.

The Power of Nice Principle #2

You never know.

OK, you're thinking. So it pays to be nice to Donald Trump's wife. But we're all smart enough to cooperate with the important people in our lives—the people we interact with often, like neighbors and coworkers, and the people involved in important transactions, such as mortgage brokers and prospective employers. We're much less likely, however, to worry about, say, a stranger whom we'll never see again. Too often, our thinking is "What does it matter?"

Diane Karnett certainly never thought the young woman she met on a train home to New York City would transform her life. The woman was visiting her grandmother, who happened to live in Diane's neighborhood, so they split a cab ride. When they arrived at the grandmother's apartment, the woman asked Diane if she'd help her carry her bags up to the fifth-floor walk-up.

"I figured why not?" But by the time they reached the fourth floor, she could think of many reasons why not.

The woman's eighty-five-year-old grandmother turned out to be an ex-Ziegfeld showgirl named Millie Darling, who befriended Diane and showed her New York as she had never known it. "Through the years, I was treated like royalty at her favorite jazz clubs and saloons," says Diane.

That would have been more than enough reward for lugging a few bags up several flights of stairs. But it turns out Millie was the mother of Chan Parker, widow of the legendary jazz great Charlie Parker. When Diane was unemployed, Chan invited Diane to live with her in her farmhouse outside of Paris. Diane accepted and told her former employer about her move. They said that since she was moving to Paris anyway, why not set up shop and run a co-venture for them there? Diane remained in Paris for four glorious years, spending weekends at Chan Parker's farmhouse, socializing with Chan's fabulous and fascinating visitors—jazz legends, journalists, even Clint Eastwood. "I could have let that stranger on the train carry her own bags up. And missed it all," says Diane.

When we meet strangers on the street, we usually assume they aren't important to us. Unlike our friend Diane, we often avoid contact with the woman sitting next to us on the train or maybe even race ahead to beat her to a cab as we exit the station. The thinking is, "She's just some woman who has nothing to do with my life. Getting the cab is more important than being nice to her."

But how do you know that? This woman could be the sister of your boss. Or a real estate agent who knows of a home in your dream neighborhood. Or the head of a foundation that could give your fledgling charity the backing it desperately needs. The bottom line is, this woman *is* important to many people. You have to treat everyone you meet as if they are the most important person in the world—because they are. If not to you, then to someone; and if not today, then perhaps tomorrow.

The Power of Nice Principle #3

People change.

One common mistake people make is assuming that you only have to be nice to your peers and their superiors.

There's no need to be nice to an assistant or receptionist, much less a security guard or a cleaning person. After all, they can't do anything for you—they have no power.

That may or may not be true—now. But you have no idea who might become quite important to you ten, twenty, or thirty years from now. A few years ago, we received a call from a woman who we thought was looking for work. We offered to meet with her, just because. As it turned out, she wasn't looking for a job—she was looking for an agency to create advertising for two huge pieces of business she was heading up. It was a project that was worth millions of dollars to the agency. Why had she picked us? Twenty-five years before, she had worked with Linda, who had shown her great kindness and respect despite her junior status at the company. More than two decades later, we ended up winning $40 million of new business because one of us had been kind to someone starting out in the advertising business. That is the power of nice.

The Power of Nice Principle #4

Nice must be automatic.

A friend recently told us the story of three consulting companies vying for a very large contract. One was summarily dropped, even though the firm did a terrific presentation. Why? they wondered. It turned out that when the prospective client arrived at the airport, an executive from one of the consulting firms neglected to help with her bags. He lost the contract right there. She was miffed at his rudeness and lack of manners, and decided that she didn't want to do business with them. Here their team had worked day and night to give the client a knockout presentation, and the entire account was lost over a suitcase.

The negligent executive certainly knew the client was a VIP. So why didn't he pick up the bag? Simple: He wasn't skilled in the art of being nice. If it had been part of the way he treated everyone, the oversight never would have occurred. Picking up the bag for the client would have been second nature, instead of a once-in-a-while gesture granted only to clients and bosses and other important people. He would have understood that such small gestures and actions can have an enormous impact.

The Power of Nice Principle #5
Negative impressions are like germs.

Whenever you're aloof to someone who you think "doesn't matter," people unconsciously react to that. You might get a better table if you scream at a waitress for service, but we can assure you that your date will silently be saying, "Check, please." Just as positive actions are like seeds, rude gestures and remarks are like germs—you may not see the impact they have on you for a while, but they are there, silently infecting you and everyone around you.

Not spreading germs means being extremely conscientious about your environment and the people around you. Because even a simple misunderstanding can create a negative impression, as Robin recently discovered:

Claire and I were up all night preparing a presentation for a client. One of the PowerPoint slides kept going in upside down. We were tear-

ing our hair out trying to get it right—it seemed to have a mind of its own. But we finally got it to work, and everyone went home.

The next day, during this presentation in a huge conference room for a lot of people, the devil slide popped onto the screen—upside down!

I said, "Oh my God, Claire. It's wrong again."

Of course, Claire knew that I was just sharing a secret joke between us—but no one else did. Everyone else thought that I had just chastised her publicly, and it created a lot of negative feeling in the room. In fact, we nearly lost the business it took months to pitch. We made light of the situation and explained what had just transpired, but it was a good lesson to us: Impressions are in the eye of the beholder, and one bad impression can infect everything else you do.

The Power of Nice Principle #6
You will know.

Even if you never see a person you have treated badly again, even if no one sees or knows of your rudeness or bad behavior, *you* will know. It will be in your mind and heart when you walk into a meeting and try to convince the people in the room that they should put their faith in you. Because you won't believe in yourself, you could jeopardize the outcome of a meeting or relationship.

The power of nice is not about running around manically smiling and doing everyone's bidding, all the while calculating what you'll get in return. It's not about being phony or manipulative. It's about valuing niceness—in yourself and in others—the same way you respect intelligence, beauty, or talent. Niceness is a powerful force. In fact, it can literally save your life.

Let us consider an example, Susan. Eight years ago, Susan received a letter from an old friend, Helen. Helen's niece was a severe anorexic; she was going to die unless she received intensive treatment in an expensive clinic thousands of miles from their home. The program cost, however, was way beyond the family's budget, given that the father was unemployed and had health problems of his own. So the family sent out a letter to family members and other friends, requesting money.

Susan was both moved and a little surprised, because people, even relatives, rarely ask for help so overtly. With three kids of her own, it was hard for Susan and her husband to decide how much to give. "We ended up sending $500—which seemed like too little and, simultaneously, way too much for us," says Susan.

But others responded generously as well. The girl was admitted into a program for treatment and survived. "Without the letter they sent, she would not have made it," says Susan.

Three years later, Susan's husband lost his job. He also suffered severe health problems. His unemployment period stretched out well over a year, and Susan's family was forced to live on savings that quickly disappeared. Even though Susan was working, they were getting very frightened about their financial situation.

Then one day a card arrived in the mail from a woman that Susan didn't know. She was Helen's mother, the anorexic girl's grandmother. She wrote that she had heard that Susan and her husband were going through a "rough patch," and that she wanted to help out. She went on to write that she knew what it was like to have financial difficulties.

"This amazing woman who had raised three children on her own working in low-paying service jobs sent us a check for $2,000," said Susan.

When you truly understand the full power of nice, you realize that by treating others with kindness, respect, and generosity, your actions get paid back in one way or another—with interest.

Now you have the principles that can help you transform your life. In the next chapters, we'll give you the tools you need to start making the power of nice work for you.

NICE CUBE

NICE CUBE: EXERCISE YOUR NICENESS MUSCLES

Every day for the next week, do five nice things that have no immediate payoff for you. Say thank you to others. Ask those you meet about their lives. Does your cleaning woman have grandchildren? Donate money to charity. Compliment a stranger.

The point of this is not to imagine that the cabdriver you are generously tipping will someday run a major corporation. It is to simply get into the habit of being nice—and rediscover how good that makes you feel.

NICE CUBE

NICE CUBE: BE A "BEST SUPPORTING ACTOR"

Most of us don't mean to be inconsiderate. We're just so busy starring in our own movie that we forget that everyone else is starring in theirs. That's why it's extremely important to see yourself as others do—as the supporting actor in *their* movie. So do an inventory of all the people in your life, and ask yourself what kind of character you'd play in their movie. Are you the loving, doting grown daughter or the distracted, absentee one? The sweet, supportive boyfriend or the needy, selfish one? The office troubleshooter or the drama queen? For each relationship, write down five ways that you can make your "character" more sympathetic.

NICE CUBE

NICE CUBE: MODEL YOURSELF AFTER THE KIND OF PERSON YOU ADMIRE

Do you admire people who do volunteer work? Who reach out to family members and make plans to do things together? Who admire and mentor others at work? Who ask about and remember the details of the lives of clients and colleagues? Complete this statement: If I were a better person, I would . . .

Try to model your behavior on that of the person you would like to be.

Chapter 3

Bake a Bigger Pie

Tony Hassini recalls the day he received a phone call from a then-unknown magician named Doug Henning. Hassini, a magician himself, possessed the blueprints for some of the world's most stunning illusions. "Henning had called several times before we were able to speak. When we did talk, I knew he was a magician who possibly might compete with me. My initial reaction was to be nice to him but not share any well-guarded secrets. I had spent ten years and a great deal of money to gather these blueprints, and I wasn't about to give them to anyone," says Hassini.

But he maintained a friendly phone relationship with Henning. "I gave him some information (nothing major) and some ideas, just to keep good relations between us," says Hassini.

It wasn't until the fifth or sixth conversation they had that Henning explained that he was working on a very different kind of magic show, a musical that would have a very intense story line around magic and—most important—would do away with the old "top hat and tails" image.

Instead, Henning would have long hair and wear brightly colored clothes. "The more I listened to him, the more I thought he had a chance of succeeding," said Hassini.

So Hassini sent Henning fourteen blueprints. "I could have charged him a good deal of money for these well-kept secrets and for my consultation. But I decided that I'd gain more from our relationship if the show was a success," says Hassini.

Of course, Hassini's gamble paid off. Henning's show opened in Toronto and broke box-office ticket records in that city. The show then moved to Broadway, where it ran for four and a half years, eventually becoming the basis for a series of phenomenally successful television specials.

Henning happily shared the pie with Hassini, offering him lucrative consulting contracts and helping him promote Tony's organization, the International Magicians Society.

The collaboration did not just enrich Henning and Hassini—it raised the profile of all magicians. Before Henning, the stereotype of the magician was a man in tuxedo and white gloves, pulling a rabbit out of a hat. Now magic was hip—which meant magicians everywhere were getting more work.

Imagine if you had been Tony Hassini when Henning started calling. Would you have given him your precious trade secrets? We're taught that the best way to succeed in life is to take as much as you can for yourself. After all, what's the first rule of a capitalist society? Beat out the competition; grab your slice of the pie before they get it first. Because if you don't, you'll be left with only crumbs. Right?

Wrong. Life is not a zero-sum game: If the other person wins, I lose, or vice versa. There's no need to squabble over who gets the biggest piece of pie—we just have to bake a bigger pie.

After all, who says the pie is finite? The universe isn't—the universe is infinite. Our capacity for love isn't finite, either, as any parent knows. You have your first child and you think your heart couldn't grow any bigger. Then you have a second child and it doubles, or triples.

Sound too airy-fairy? Well, consider how the Internet has expanded opportunities for everyone. It used to be that when you needed a new job, your options were limited—you could search the want ads in the newspaper, visit an employment agency, maybe put the word out to a few friends. Now you have a vast array of resources: There are job-hunting Web sites like monster.com and networking sites like xanga.com. Every major company has a "career opportunities" section on its Web site that you can access in a few keystrokes. Or you can just e-mail your résumé to choice contacts, asking them to forward it, and as the old commercial goes, "They tell two friends, and they tell two friends, and so on and so on." The Internet has given everyone a vastly expanded network. No one has to "lose" contacts—the pool is deeper for everyone.

And the more people you include, the better off you are. Supermodel-turned-entrepreneur Kathy Ireland realized this after she was asked to do a public-service announcement for prenatal care. She agreed to do so free of charge—as long as they also allowed her to tape a spot in Spanish. "My husband works in an emergency room and speaks Spanish out of necessity—he has to be able to give Spanish-speaking patients critical information. So I told them that I wanted to do the PSA in Spanish as well as English, because this is really important information. We can't let people miss out on this," says Kathy.

Kathy did the bilingual taping because it was the right thing to do—she didn't have a business motive. But after the announcement aired, she was astonished to see how people in the Latino community responded to the spot—and how it affected their interest in her clothing line. "It was incredible. Our Latina customers responded in such a powerful way. They wrote letters and e-mails saying that they were so grateful for the PSA. It made us realize how underserved they had been," she says.

As a result, Kathy's company made a more concerted effort to reach out to its Latina customers—for example, by printing their hangtags in both Spanish and English. "This has helped our brand in such a powerful way. We realized that our customers felt isolated and ignored, and now that we've reached out to them they've really embraced the brand."

Baking a bigger pie is the ultimate win-win situation. You get more of what you want and feel better about what you're doing. So instead of expending all that negative energy rushing to grab that slice first, think about how you can broaden your horizons and create a new recipe for success.

HELP OTHER PEOPLE GET THEIR SLICE

When you're desperate to get your slice of the pie, why would you be interested in helping other people get their piece?

Had Ernest Hamwi taken that attitude when he was selling zalabia, a very thin Persian waffle, at the 1904 World's

Fair, he might have ended his days as a street vendor. Hamwi noticed that a nearby ice-cream vendor ran out of bowls to serve to his customers. Most people would have sniffed, "Not my problem," perhaps even hoping the ice-cream vendor's misfortune would mean more customers for him. Instead, Hamwi rolled up a waffle and plopped a scoop of ice cream on top, creating one of the world's first ice-cream cones. He helped his neighbor—and, in the process, made a fortune.

That's the beauty of helping other people to get theirs—you often help create a bigger pie in the bargain. By choosing to mentor a young person, you might discover some ideas about business that will help clarify your own goals and values. When Shira Miller was the marketing director for a large food and nutrition company, she noticed that one of her sales support specialists had enormous talent. So Miller brought her into the public relations department and helped her develop her skills. After Miller left the company to start her own PR firm, she continued to offer her friend advice and career-development tips. Now Miller's protégée is the director of corporate communications for Focus Brands, the parent company of Carvel Ice Cream and Cinnabon—and Carvel is currently one of Miller's strongest clients. "Mentoring and developing my employees is something that has always brought me great personal satisfaction. But I had no idea it would also bring me clients!" says Miller.

POOL YOUR RESOURCES

Sometimes we're so focused on holding on to what we have—customers, contacts, ideas—that we forget that pooling resources with other people, teams, or businesses may actually result in a far greater profit for everyone.

Executives at The Breast Cancer Research Foundation (BCRF) discovered this after a disappointing fund-raiser. BCRF was the founding charity partner of a consumer loyalty/fund-raising program called "The Cure Card." For $25, customers bought the card, which entitled them to discounts at various merchants. Half the proceeds of the card were donated to the foundation. The program was very successful, but the next year new retailers didn't sign up.

So they made an unusual move—they decided to team up with The Susan G. Komen Breast Cancer Foundation. This meant swallowing a good deal of pride—even though they were working on behalf of the same good cause, they were still competing for a share of the wallet. A new card, the "Love Cures" card, was created, which drew a large retail partner and had great sales. Of course, the best news is that they raised more money for breast cancer. Even after splitting the pot with the Komen Foundation, The Breast Cancer Research Foundation made more money than if they had worked solo.

When you learn to shed the "me vs. you" mentality, you open up opportunities for everyone. For example, not long ago Procter & Gamble executives realized there was no reason to shut out former employees. "Historically, when people left Procter & Gamble, they were shunned. They cut the cord and were no longer part of the family," says P&G's Charlotte Otto. Nevertheless, many former P&G staffers maintained contact with one another, creating informal "alumni" networks. But it wasn't until A. G. Lafley became CEO that the company started officially participating in the reunions. Lafley realized that its former employees weren't traitors—to the contrary, they were extremely valuable allies. "We have benefited greatly from much stronger connections with alums," says Otto. P&G alum Brent Bailey went on to become the president and COO of Pharmavite, which is best known for its Nature Made and Nature's Resource vitamins and supplements. In 2003, Bailey facilitated a deal in which Procter & Gamble licensed their Olay brand to the company, creating the very successful Olay Vitamin brand.

By sharing information and insights, you can frequently collaborate in ways in which the sum is far greater than the individual parts. Think about the collective power of the Beatles. After the band broke up, John, Paul, George, and Ringo went on to have very respectable musical careers. But none of them ever came close to the legendary success of the Fab Four. Light-opera superstars Gilbert and Sullivan reportedly couldn't stand each other personally, but together they wrote some of the world's greatest comic operas. When they tried on their own, they were failures.

And, of course, some of the world's most successful products were created this way. Daniel Peter, the Swiss chocolatier, spent years trying to find a way to add milk to lighten the texture and taste of his chocolates—regular milk didn't mix well with cocoa paste. Then he met Henri Nestlé, a pharmacist who had created a sweetened condensed milk for infant formula. It turned out to be just the thing Peter needed. And the rest of us have been enjoying milk chocolate ever since.

Sometimes, great collaborations are years in the making. For example, when Dr. Spence Silver created the glue for

Post-its, he thought it was a failure. Silver was trying to create an ultrastrong adhesive for his employer, 3M, and instead discovered a very weak glue that would stick to most anything, but was easily peeled off. The invention sat on a shelf for five years. Then one day Silver's coworker, Art Fry, was practicing for his church choir and was frustrated because his paper markers kept falling out. He remembered Silver's adhesive, stuck it on a slip of paper and—eureka!—the Post-it was born.

SPREAD THE WEALTH

We tend to think of the natural world as being harsh and cutthroat, and ruthless. Behavior in the business world is often ruled by "The law of the jungle." But cooperation is as much a successful strategy for the boardroom as it is for hunting down prey.

Consider the vampire bat. In *The Origins of Virtue,* author Matt Ridley describes how vampire bats search for large animals with cuts and open wounds—the source of their daily meal. Now, vampire bats may not be warm and fuzzy creatures. But they know how to share. When a bat finds a good source of food, it's unable to take in more than it needs, so it shares its food source with another bat. Its generosity will be rewarded when it has a bad day finding its prey. The bat that refuses to share quickly learns that it will be denied blood when it needs it. Vampire bats cannot survive unless they share.

Sharing food has been a central feature of nearly every human society, as well. After all, it makes sense: The caveman who bagged a mammoth couldn't eat the whole thing;

he might as well share it and ensure that he gets to eat when someone else gets a score.

We no longer rely on our next-door neighbor for our next meal, but an instinct to share and cooperate is part of every civilization. If bats can keep tabs on who is cooperating and who is not, you can be sure that your friends and coworkers are doing the same.

And as talk-show host Jay Leno points out, hoarding everything for yourself is ultimately unsatisfying. "If you ate a whole pie, you'd make yourself sick. You eat as much pie as you want and then whatever's left you give to other people," says Leno. When Jay celebrated his tenth anniversary on *The Tonight Show,* he found a way to share his success with others on the show—he gave each staffer $1,000 for every year they had worked on the show, out of his own bank account. It might not sound like much unless you know that there are 175 people on the show. Everyone from clerical workers to producers received this bonus. That gives it a lot of meaning. Someone who had been with the show for eight years received an $8,000 bonus. "Rather than just saying 'thank you,' you're giving them something that means something," says Leno.

For Yvon Chouinard, the founder of the outdoor-gear company Patagonia, sharing the pie means offering his employees the same benefits that made him want to start up his own company. "We have a policy here—it's called 'Let My People Go Surfing.' A policy which is, when the surf comes up, anybody can just go surfing. . . . That attitude changes your whole life," Chouinard told psychologist Mihaly Csikszentmihalyi in *Good Business: Leadership, Flow, and the Making of Meaning.*

We would argue that Leno and Chouinard aren't just playing Santa. They're making very shrewd business decisions. The No. 1 reason that Americans quit their jobs is that they don't feel appreciated, according to the U.S. Department of Labor.[1] When you consider that the average cost to a company for a manager or a professional who leaves is eighteen months' worth of salary, flexible surfing hours or a once-in-a-decade bonus are bargains![2]

SHARE THE CREDIT

When we created our agency, we wanted to show the world, and our naysayers, that we could create a very successful company and still come home and have dinner with our families. How did we do this? We learned to relax. We try not to worry about who gets the credit—we just want to keep building our business, expanding the pie. Not surprisingly, this attitude has helped us to work better. As Harry Truman once said, "It is amazing what you can accomplish if you do not care who gets the credit."

We all want to be recognized for our achievements. In the back of our mind, many of us have an imaginary audience that applauds or jeers us for our successes or failures. But we would argue this is counterproductive. For one thing, there is no audience; everyone's too engrossed in their own drama to even begin to worry about you. In the words of eleventh-century Buddhist scholar Atisha Dipankara, "Don't expect applause."

Second, when you let others share the ownership of an idea, you create a community of people who will help to nurture and grow those ideas into something far greater than you ever imagined. Who cares if ten people think the idea is "theirs"? The end result will likely be ten times more exciting than if you take all the credit.

DON'T WORRY ABOUT MAKING A BIG STATEMENT

When Jennifer joined a citizen-advocacy group in her hometown, Savannah, Georgia, she didn't set out to change the world. She joined because she believed in the organization's mission: to help the developmentally disabled, one person at a time. Jennifer was matched with Wendi, who had Hurler's syndrome, a terribly debilitating and terminal developmental disorder. A waiver issued by the state of Georgia enabled Wendi to get the extensive nursing care she needed in her home. But when Wendi turned ten, the state canceled her waiver. "They were going to put her in a nursing home in Florida, where she would have no contact with her mother, brother, or grandparents," said Jennifer.

Because Wendi's single mother worked in a factory and couldn't make phone calls during the day, Jennifer became Wendi's advocate, calling state authorities and pleading her case. Finally, Jennifer and Wendi's family testified before the Medicaid oversight board in Atlanta and successfully maintained Wendi's at-home care.

Helping one sick child is unquestionably a wonderful accomplishment. But in doing so, Jennifer also helped countless other disabled kids. It turns out that the testimony of Wendi's friends and family helped extend Medicaid waivers throughout the United States.

When you start helping other people get their slice of the

pie, you don't have to set out with a grand purpose. You don't need to change the world. But by dedicating yourself to baking a bigger pie, you'll find there is no limit to what you can do.

NICE CUBE

NICE CUBE: HOLD A NETWORKING PARTY

Hold a networking get-together where you invite people from completely different industries—your sister who owns a B & B, the software engineer you went to college with, a friend who works at the local newspaper. Select people who you believe would enjoy one another's company (i.e., not the passive-aggressive nerd from Accounts Receivable). But beyond that, don't fashion any agenda other than providing a nice time for your guests. Then sit back and see what materializes over the course of the evening. You might find that your friend who works in a flower shop is able to give your innkeeper sister tips on how to attract more wedding business—and perhaps provide the flowers!

NICE CUBE

NICE CUBE: MAKE A DIFFERENCE

As the Beatles said, "And, in the end, the pie you take, is equal to the pie you bake." OK, that's not exactly what they said, but you get the point. In other words, every time someone gives you an idea, a job tip, or a loan—make sure to pass it on. It doesn't have to be an exact quid pro quo. If someone higher up in your company gives you some good advice, think about passing it on to a more junior person you would like to mentor. If a competitor recommends you for a job she can't take, try to come back to her with some worthwhile contacts. Or just do something nice. Visit a home for the aged. Or call your grandmother, for goodness' sake—she's dying to hear from you!

NICE CUBE

NICE CUBE: THROW OUT THE SCORECARD

Whether we acknowledge it or not, most of us keep a running tally of what we have and compare it to what other people we know have. My sister has a new baby, but I have a more active social life. My best friend makes more money, but I have a more interesting job. We keep running tallies and mostly feel fine—as long as things stay roughly equal. Why not toss out the scorecard and just live our lives without it—without somehow believing that someone else's success means our failure. Well, you can. Whenever you feel as if you've lost out relative to someone else, give them more. If you're burning with envy over someone else's promotion, send her flowers. If your sister just purchased a palatial country home, make her dinner at your apartment. Why? you ask. When you start acting from a place of abundance, you'll start to feel that sense of abundance. Once you start to experience that richness, you won't worry so much about what the Joneses have.

Chapter 4

Sweeten the Deal

While traveling on a business trip from Los Angeles to New York, Rachel Pine noticed that the airline crew looked extremely harried. So when the flight attendant came by to check her seat belt, Rachel offered her a Fig Newton from her family-size pack. "She took it, and was so grateful that she looked like she was going to burst into tears," said Rachel. Soon after, the attendant returned and asked Rachel to follow her—to first class. "The attendant said, 'You have no idea what our last flight was like. If just one passenger had been like you, it would have been bearable.'"

From Fig Newton to first class—it's surprising how big an impact a sweet gesture or remark can have. To taste success in more areas of your life, sprinkle a bit of sugar now and then. Boosting the morale of the people around you can reap some outsized rewards. Research by psychologists David G. Myers and Ruut Veenhoven has shown that people who are in a good mood are more likely to help others; employees in a cheerful mood are more likely to judge a job-interview candidate favorably than people in a bad mood.[1] That probably rings true with your own experience. The fact is, we all respond favorably when kindness is extended to us. Moreover, research has found that the happier an employee is, the more productive and creative he or she will be. "Feeling good lubricates mental efficiency, making people better at understanding information and using decision rules in complex judgments," writes psychologist Daniel Goleman in his bestselling book *Primal Leadership*. Goleman found that positive feelings in the workplace also make employees behave more ethically and function more cooperatively in teams. And because they are happier, they are less likely to take a job with another company.

The next time you meet with a new client—or an old friend, for that matter—why not start off by complimenting his appearance or her outfit? We sometimes forget to establish a rapport with the other person before launching into the business at hand or the topic we want to discuss. To tweak an old adage, you'll capture more money with honey than a bland old pie chart. In every encounter, only 7 percent of our communication is verbal. The other 93 percent comes from nonverbal cues such as gestures and tone of voice. People seldom remember who gave the pithier speech in a business meeting—but they do remember who smiled more, and who expressed concern for them.

LET 'EM EAT CAKE

Gail was a freelance graphic designer with the typical self-employed person's problem: lots of work, but little money coming in. Although her business was brisk and her billings were high, her clients simply weren't paying their bills. "My money seemed stuck in their bank accounts," says Gail.

Gail tried a number of tactics to convince her creditors to pay—from letters that said "Please pay soon" festooned with smiley faces to diplomatic phone calls—but nothing worked. Desperate, she stumbled on what turned out to be a brilliantly effective idea: bribing them with baked goods. "I would send out reminders of past-due invoices with the enticement that if paid by a specified date, I would reward the client with fresh baked cookies, brownies, cake—whatever they wanted. And it worked."

We often act as if business is very complicated, convincing ourselves that our policies have to be ultrarational and our approach high-tech. We focus on our negotiating techniques and intellectual prowess. We carry on about our skill sets or drop the name of the prestigious business school we attended. We forget that sometimes a simple inducement or reward can trump the most sophisticated systems. Having an MBA from Harvard or Wharton is fine, but there are times when a fancy degree just can't match a simple glass of ice-cold lemonade.

Or a Cherry Coke. Before interviewing Warren Buffett for a radio commercial for the New York Stock Exchange, Linda read in his bio that he loved Cherry Coke anytime of the day or night. He'd also made a killing on Coca-Cola stock—which usually gives a person a warm and fuzzy feeling about any brand. So right before the interview, Warren was treated to his favorite soft drink. He looked at the can and smiled. "Linda," he said, "I'll tell you anything you want to know, because you just brought me a Cherry Coke."

What did that soda cost—a dollar? Yet that simple gesture resulted in access to one of the most brilliant minds in business.

The next time someone close to you is feeling cranky or disagreeable, try handing them a few chocolate Kisses or offering them the candy bowl. Although scientists haven't completely unraveled the mysteries of chocolate, they do know that it contains several organic compounds that produce feelings of well-being in the human brain. The tryptophan found in chocolate, for example, enables the brain to create serotonin, an organic compound that can produce feelings of elation and ecstasy. And the phenylethylamine in chocolate stimulates the brain's pleasure centers and produces many of the feelings of infatuation, including giddiness, attraction, and excitement.[2]

Of course, you don't have to be a biologist or chemist to figure this out. It was one of our talented art directors, Whitney Pillsbury, who suggested giving clients chocolate. He mentioned that we always seemed to enjoy his ideas more while we were munching on the M&Ms he brought to our meetings. Several pounds later, we started using this delicious ploy with our clients, lavishing them with sweets before we presented our work. Whether because of the sweets or our hospitality, our clients seemed more receptive to some of our "out of the box" thinking. We've now expanded our offerings to include brownies, cookies, and Godiva truffles (for the really difficult accounts!).

TICKLE THEIR FUNNY BONE

Each morning at the Electrical Products of India company, the employees gather together to laugh. Managers at the company told employment consultant Michael Kerr that the daily yuk session has increased productivity, improved employee relationships, and reduced stress-related illness, including headaches and colds.

It might sound silly, but Daniel Goleman says that research on humor finds that workplace jokes and laughter help to stimulate employee creativity and improve communication and trust. In a negotiation, the casual exchange of jocular banter increases the likelihood of financial concessions.

Afraid that making jokes at work might prevent you from being taken seriously? Think again. Goleman's research shows that leaders who were considered outstanding (based on financial performance and ratings by peers and bosses) tended to make three times more witty remarks than executives with average ratings. That doesn't mean you need to start rehearsing a stand up routine or start wearing a clown outfit to work on Casual Friday.

As Goleman notes, the most effective corporate humor comes not from canned jokes but from friendly banter and situational humor.

SPREAD THE SUGAR

Helene Stapinski was sitting in a toney Los Angeles restaurant, waiting to do a reading of her first book, a memoir called *Five-Finger Discount*. She had been nervous before the reading started, but now she was terrified. The person who was reading right before her was brilliant, a well-known character actor who read a hysterical piece that had the audience howling with laughter. Helene was laughing, too, but she was also a wreck. "I kept thinking, 'How can I possibly follow this guy?' It was a complete nightmare," says Helene. After all, Helene's book had lots of jokes and funny parts, but it was never intended to be stand-up comedy.

But when she got up to read, Helene discovered that she'd never had a more receptive or appreciative audience. "They laughed at stuff no other audience had laughed at before—stuff that *I* never even thought was funny," said Helene.

Helene discovered something that professional comedians know well—audiences don't have a finite amount of good cheer. To the contrary, the better the opening act, the more they'll like the act that follows. That's why theaters use a warm-up act before the star attraction goes on. Anyone who has attended a live taping of a late-night program like *The Tonight Show* or *The Late Show* knows that the real performance doesn't begin with Jay or Dave's monologue. A comedian performs for the live studio audience before the cameras start rolling, to warm them up before Leno or Letterman takes the stage. The producers know that the opening act doesn't "use up" the laughter; rather, it primes the pump, so that the audience's laughter flows more easily.

As a Talmudic scholar once said, we can't get more if we don't give out what we have. We all have a cup of sugar inside us, so why not dole it out a bit? You'll find that your supply is replenished many times over.

FLASH A SMILE

Think about the last time you played with a baby. When you put your hands over your eyes, she did the same thing. "Mirroring" is a natural human behavior. Through imitation, our species is able to learn, communicate, and empathize. Our natural inclination for mimicry means that we often "catch" each other's moods, which is why you might start to feel anxious when your husband starts stressing about seeing his mother, or why an easygoing, buoyant new hire can change the energy in an office.

The good news is that positive emotions are more contagious than negative ones. A Yale University School of Management study found that cheerfulness and warmth spread far more quickly throughout an office than irritability and depression. The best way to spread these good feelings? With a big toothy smile, the most contagious gesture of all.

Linda realized this after splurging on some cosmetic dentistry:

Ever since I was a kid, I never had the perfectly straight teeth I saw in magazines. So I grew up without smiling a whole lot. I just hated my teeth. Then I had laminates put in, and three months later had the gleaming pearly whites I'd always dreamt about. I now had a lot *to smile about and started grinning all the time. When my husband took the garbage out, I broke into a broad grin. When my assistant handed me my morning Starbucks, I would flash her a dazzling smile of appreciation. Short of attending an elderly aunt's funeral, I found every encounter an excuse to smile. The result: Everyone around me began to smile with me. Client meetings became more amicable, negotiations became nicer, coworkers felt more appreciated. And the best result? A year later, Robin went to the same dentist, Dr. Robert Sorin, and now I have the happiest business partner imaginable.*

When you smile at others, you literally "infect" them with happiness. Psychologist Fritz Stack discovered this when he had participants in a study hold a pencil with their teeth, which activated the smiling muscles. When they were smiling, participants found cartoons funnier than when they weren't smiling. Translation: It's a lot easier to make your client, your boss, or your husband more receptive to your ideas if you say it with a smile.

OFFER A GIFT

Ever wonder why car dealers so often give you flowers or even DVD players after you've purchased a new vehicle? The reason is simple: The little gift will make you enjoy the big-ticket item more. Studies have shown that customers who were given a present after making a major purchase, like a car or a television, reported more satisfaction with the product than customers who were not given a gift.[3]

Our friend Geraldine Laybourne, the CEO and founder of the Oxygen network and a pioneer in the cable-television industry, discovered this when she was trying to get her network picked up by EchoStar Communications, operator of the DISH Network satellite TV. "We had been working on the deal for years, and we came close many times," says Laybourne. But it always fell through. Laybourne was frustrated, but she maintained a friendly relationship with EchoStar's CEO, Charlie Ergen, corresponding with him by e-mail and visiting EchoStar with other Oxygen staffers to offer insights on the female viewer. But perhaps Laybourne's most inspired move was the simplest. After EchoStar launched an ad campaign in which pigs were featured prominently, Laybourne's office showered him with pork products—precooked bacon on Monday, ham on

Tuesday, spareribs on Wednesday, and a note that said, "Spare yourself any more pig parts, sign up Oxygen."

Ergen appreciated the gifts, but there was still no deal. "It didn't work, but he saw that we were creative—always positive, always fun." Then, about two years later, EchoStar had a contentious rate-increase dispute with another women's network. EchoStar staffers immediately called Oxygen. "They said they wanted to be in business with us because we were positive, and even though we were frustrated at times, we always took the 'nice' approach and continued to try harder," says Laybourne. At the beginning of 2006, Oxygen had a contract with EchoStar to be in at least 7 million homes. A little bit of bacon can go a long way.

OFFER COMPLIMENTS

A young man once asked Abraham Lincoln if it was irritating to constantly be asked for autographs. "Men will stand a good deal when they are flattered," the president replied.

Lincoln's words are as true now as they were in his day. We all love a compliment. And yet so often we're slow to give them to each other. Linda recalls:

When I was working at another agency, I bought myself a beautiful new suit. I was really proud of it. I had just had a baby and was trying to get my weight back, and I felt so good in this suit. But all day, no one said anything to me about it. I felt incredibly disappointed. Finally, I asked one of my colleagues why no one had mentioned my suit. He looked at me dryly and said, "It's called a law *suit."*

In other words, people were *afraid* to offer their coworkers and acquaintances even the most innocent compliments—afraid that a kind word about another person's blouse or hairstyle might be taken the wrong way. We all need to lighten up. If you consistently tell your twenty-years-younger assistant what great pecs he has, then sure, you might hear some complaints. But for the most part, telling a fellow human being that they look nice or that they have a magnetic personality will almost always go over extremely well.

Some people refrain from compliments because they're afraid that they will come off as phony or smarmy.

But let us tell you something: If you're concerned that a compliment will come off as phony or patronizing, then almost certainly it won't. The very fact that you're worried about it means you aren't a slick glad-hander, and you won't come off that way.

But what if you are a lovable curmudgeon who would shock your friends and colleagues if you suddenly started handing out chocolates and complimenting their hair? Well, the great thing about sweetening your surroundings is that it only takes a pinch of sugar to do so. And if you're known as a crank, any praise or laughter from you will be even more meaningful. Karen, the president of a medium-sized company, had a quick temper. When she became stressed out, she would snap at those around her. She tried to control her comments and behavior, but in the heat of the moment she just couldn't help it.

So Karen learned to make up for it. First, she always apologized when her temper got the better of her. More important, she made it a regular part of her day to praise her employees—and not just offer them a "nice job." One of Karen's former employees said, "When you did something right, Karen made you feel like the smartest, most talented person in the world. She'd go nuts praising you, and it would fortify you for the times when she was mean or critical. You could take it, because she had built up your confidence so much before."

Karen stayed true to her salty personality, while offering up the kinder comments that her staff needed. The power of nice is about being *kind*, not *phony*.

NICE CUBE

NICE CUBE: FLASH A SMILE

Studies show that the simple act of smiling will actually make you feel happier, as it will the people around you. So try getting into the habit of smiling more. For practice, smile at strangers you see on the street. If you live in a crowded city, where people are constantly whizzing by, pick one person on every city block. Start with children, or even dogs. Then smile at adults who look friendly and receptive. After a time, you'll be ready to smile at even the most crabby-looking person. He or she may or may not return the favor, but that's not the point. You want to get to the point where smiling is as natural for you as breathing.

NICE CUBE

NICE CUBE: MIMIC THE MASTERS

You don't have to be a professional comedian to get a laugh out of people, but watching them can help. Study your favorite comedy movies or TV shows; memorize not just the jokes but the timing and cadence. Then repeat them to friends and colleagues. The point is not to steal material—you can always credit the joke as you're telling it—but to practice making others laugh. (Of course, it's not a bad thing to become associated with the wit and wisdom of a Jon Stewart or a Will Ferrell, either.) A note of caution: This habit can lead to overkill. If you're constantly mimicking the nasal voice of your favorite *Saturday Night Live* character, your colleagues' amusement will wane quickly.

NICE CUBE

NICE CUBE: OFFER A SWEET

Keep a stash of fun-sized candy bars on your desk or nearby. When the people who come to see you seem tense, tired, or cranky, pop open your drawer and pass out the Snickers. (Note: Extra credit for homemade cookies.)

Chapter 5

Help Your Enemies

When Marla started working in the television industry, she had a terrible boss. "He literally believed in working his staff to the breaking point. People would quit from exhaustion, and he'd just hire a new batch," says Marla. He was such a slave driver that at one point he had a nurse come in with free B_{12} shots to keep his people healthy so they would work more.

In the intervening years, Marla moved from the development side of the business to the production side; she was now a senior executive at one of the major Hollywood studios. You can imagine the surprise Marla felt when, years later, she learned that her former boss would now be pitching *her.* In a complete turn of the tables, it was she who had the power to accept or reject her ex-boss's project. "Oh the delight! The thrill! The chilling potential of doing unto him as he had done unto me and everyone else on his staff! But then I heard my mother's voice in the back of my head: *Kill him with kindness.*" So that's exactly what she did. "You could see the suspicion in his eyes when I offered to get him coffee, instead of sending my assistant to get it. He got really nervous when I asked about his children," she says. "And then, during the pitch, I let him present with all his heart, while I listened intently."

To Marla's relief, the idea was terrible, making it easy for her to reject it honestly. But she wrote him a polite note, thanking him for his time and letting him know he was always welcome to pitch her again.

Years later, Marla found herself working on a very big television deal. "I absolutely adored this project. I knew that if I could get the rights to the project, it would bring my career to the next level," says Marla. So she was floored when she realized whom she'd be pitching—her old boss! "He was in the power seat this time, but by overwhelming him with kindness, I had turned the tables on the relationship," says Marla. "While I'm sure he's never going to win any Emily Post awards, he did show me proper respect and—most important—he agreed to the deal I needed! I was never so glad that I listened to Mama's words and resisted the impulse for revenge."

Marla had embraced a principle that has helped us tremendously throughout our careers and our lives: Helping your opponent can be one of the most valuable things you can do for yourself.

We live in a zero-sum culture. In any given year, there can only be one president, one Oscar winner for best picture, one gold-medal-winning decathlete. But although these events get the front-page headlines, most of life is not that black and white. There are very few women who will get the award for "Best Suburban Wife in a Supporting Role."

Our culture urges us to pit ourselves against one another. Businesspeople read trade journals to find out how their company stacks up against their competitors. Parents engage in fierce battles to get their kids into the best preschools. We view the people who are going after the same things we are as the enemy. That's why when we hear about others' good fortune we sometimes find ourselves feeling a bit deflated. When we see the competition is doing badly, we sometimes feel a wicked delight.

But who is the enemy, anyway? There are very few individuals in this world whom we could really identify as enemies. We'll give you Osama bin Laden, but most of the people we consider "enemies" are really just people who wound our egos, like the coworker who beats you out of a promotion or the boyfriend who had the nerve to leave you. That's why divorce can get so ugly. Nobody really cares who gets the CD collection of Barry Manilow's greatest hits—the ex-spouses are just lashing out because their pride has been wounded.

When you learn to let go of your pride and stop keeping score, you'll find that actually you'll do much better. Because most of life isn't me vs. you. Most of the time, we work in teams. We cooperate. That's what civilizations are all about. There may be one president, but it takes 535 members of Congress to run our legislative branch. You and your coworker may engage in a friendly competition about who has a better sales record, but the bottom line is that you'll both need to do well if you want your company's revenues, and stock price, to rise.

The way the cast of the hit TV show *Friends* renewed their contracts offers a great example of this. The cast realized they could increase their negotiating power—and their bank-account balances—if they negotiated their salaries as a group, with each actor receiving the same pay. They could have gotten into a big ego war about whether Jennifer Aniston or Lisa Kudrow was the star of the show. Instead, they put down the scorecard and extended the life of the show. And, of course, made a killing!

WHY COOPERATION BEATS OUT THE COMPETITION

To better understand why cooperation is such a powerful strategy, think about a familiar psychological experiment called "The Prisoner's Dilemma." In the experiment, there are two players and a banker. Each player is given two cards. One card says "cooperate" and one says "defect." Each player has to decide whether or not to cooperate, without knowing what the other player will do. If both players cooperate, they each receive $300. If they both defect, they are each fined $10. So there is incentive to cooperate, *if the other player makes the same choice.* However, if one player cooperates and the other defects, then the defector wins $500 and the cooperator receives the "sucker's payoff"—a $100 fine.

Initially, it might seem like defecting is the best choice, since it carries both the highest reward and the lowest penalty. In fact, defecting is the best choice—*if you only play the game once.* But researchers found that when people played the game multiple times, they started cooperating. The game is self-policing—no one can defect for very long without the other player punishing them by defecting as well. The players quickly figure out that the best strategy to ensure success is to forgo the big $500 reward and instead consistently go for the $300.[1]

Anyone who has ever bought or sold something on eBay understands this principle. Say you're trying to sell your grandmother's antique vase, which is beautiful but has a large chip in the back. If you neglect to mention the chip in your listing, you'll get a higher price for the vase. However, if you do that you can forget about trying to sell anything else on the site, because eBay has created a way to punish cheaters and reward cooperators—the feedback form. Buyers and sellers routinely post evaluations of their transactions, saying whether they thought the other party was honest and nice to work with. The person who received the damaged vase would no doubt report that you had misrepresented it, and you'd find very few people interested in doing business with you again.

In eBay and in life, defecting works only in the short term. Because in most of life, you don't deal with others just once. What do we do before we meet a potential new business partner or blind date? We Google them. In our age of instant information, you simply can't get away with treating others badly. By the same token, our instant communication system can also help someone with a sterling reputation impress both friends and foes.

Below are some of the strategies we've learned over the years to cooperate with others, and turn even enemies into allies and friends.

SKATE YOUR BEST PROGRAM

As an avid ice skater, Robin knows that the best way to win is to skate your best program. Skaters know that it's never in their best interest to look at the competition, because there is nothing you can do to change how well or badly someone else skates. You can win only on your own performance. Any time spent thinking "Well, she's going to do this, so I'll do that" is just wasted energy. It wears down your confidence. And the truth is, if your competitor falls on her double axel, it won't help you land one.

There is a finite amount of energy each of us has to expend every day. So how do you want to use that energy—perfecting your game or trying to tear down someone else's? Every time you get into the ring with an adversary, you are taking your eye off the prize. Spending all your time fighting with someone is the quickest way to lose business, because you are no longer trying to build something up. You're expending your energy tearing someone down. It's exhausting, and it leads nowhere.

We discovered just how well the ice-skating rule applies to business when a major food company invited The Kaplan Thaler Group and another agency to bid for some new business.

The client wanted us to work collaboratively and share information. So we attended brainstorming and research sessions together, although we developed our campaigns separately, since we were competing against each other for the work. But here was the kicker: The client wanted one person to coordinate the flow of information—making sure everyone got all the various e-mails, faxes, meeting schedules, and so on, and they gave that responsibility to Robin:

Of course, I was supposed to be objective, but how could I be completely? I had the power to choose the information I'd share with the other team. I could decide which meetings they were included in—

and which ones they were not. All it would take was a "Whoops! You didn't get my e-mail? How strange!"

We were very nervous about winning the account; the people at the other agency were very smart and talented. But we made a critical decision on Day One. We could not afford to spend one second diverting our attention away from the job. Any time spent trying to figure out how to outsmart our competition or outmaneuver them politically would do nothing but increase our chances of losing. So we shared all the information we received and invited them to all the meetings.

We also kept our mouths shut when we heard that one of their executives flew out to the client's West Coast office for a "secret meeting" with the executive vice president. We put the politics out of our minds and just kept working.

Then the moment of truth: We got the call and won the business hands down. Even though the other company had a strong prior relationship with the client, in the end it was the work—not the politics—that got us the job. We also won the client's admiration for our ability to work so well with a competitor.

Granted, there are times when having an adversary can help spur you on. It's true that racers run faster in competition than in practice. But even in a neck-and-neck race, there is a "nice" way to behave. Think about the famous collision between Mary Decker and Zola Budd in the women's 3,000-meter final at the 1984 Summer Olympics. American Mary Decker was the favorite to win the race, but South African-born Zola Budd, who was running for Britain, was also a serious contender. At the 1,700-meter mark, Budd inadvertently cut off Decker, causing her to fall. Budd kept running, while Decker lay on the track in tears. Budd came in seventh while the audience booed. She never recovered her damaged reputation. Think how different Budd's life would have been if, in that split second, she had stopped and tried to help Decker up? She wouldn't have won the gold, but she would have been a hero throughout the world.

COMPLIMENT THE COMPETITION

At a 2005 National Press Club panel, Newt Gingrich was heard praising Senator Hillary Clinton, saying things like "Senator Clinton is exactly right" and "Hillary is so correct in the direction that she laid out."[2]

What gives? In the mid-nineties, Gingrich, as majority leader of the House, lacerated Clinton's health-care proposals and called for the impeachment of her husband. Now suddenly they're best buddies?

It turns out the two former rivals agree on many issues of health-care policy and military preparedness. What better way to get their message out than to turn heads with their odd-couple pairing?

Newt and Hillary realized that on these issues working together was more profitable than tearing down the competition. And while we don't kid ourselves that this signals a permanent détente between the Democrats and the Republicans, if Newt and Hillary can work together at least some of the time, surely we can all look for common ground with our own so-called enemies.

The top brass at Sony and Samsung have realized this, as well. The two electronics manufacturers have been in fierce competition for years. In fact, the success of these two companies is a point of national pride for Japan and Korea, their respective countries. As a result, many were surprised when the two companies started working *together* to create flat-screen televisions. The heads of both companies decided that each could benefit from the other company's strengths. Samsung has more advanced technologies, but Sony is more skilled at applying those technologies to consumer goods. Working together, both companies are improving the quality of all their products.[3]

Once you get past the idea that for every winner there must be a loser, amazing things can happen. Look at the Three Tenors. The opera world is known for its divas; who could have imagined that you could get the three biggest stars in opera together on one stage? But when Luciano Pavarotti, Placido Domingo, and José Carreras shared the spotlight, they only increased their fame, creating the best-selling classical music album in history.

TREAT TODAY'S ADVERSARIES LIKE TOMORROW'S ALLIES

During the Revolutionary War, George Washington insisted that his soldiers treat their prisoners well. Even the prisoners themselves were shocked to receive such humane treatment. In *Washington's Crossing,* historian David Hackett Fischer quotes one of Washington's orders to Lieutenant Colonel Samuel Blachley Webb: "You are to take charge of privates of the British Army . . . Treat them with humanity, and Let them have no Reason to Complain of our Copying the brutal example of the British army in their

Treatment of our unfortunate brethren . . . Provide everything necessary for them on the road."

Washington was not merely being a stand-up guy. He knew that these prisoners were potentially among the first citizens of the fledgling United States of America. He wanted them to come over to the colonists' side. And after the war, that's exactly what many of them did.

The father of our country was a lot more forward thinking than most of us. Because in our highly competitive culture, it's easy to forget that people switch teams all the time. Your favorite hometown baseball player signs as a free agent for the team's archrival. Your best friend at the office used to work for the company's direct competitor. Yet we still stomp around acting like our adversaries will be our bitter enemies forevermore.

In the real world, the adversary-ally relationship is forever in flux. For example, in our business, we compete directly against other agencies to get work. But we've also learned that these agencies can be very valuable friends. So even though we vie against one another for certain accounts, we also frequently help one another with leads on accounts we can't compete for. Our friends at Leo Burnett referred us to U.S. Bank when they were unable to go after that business. We referred an airline to our friend Kevin Roberts at Saatchi, since we already have the Continental Airlines account.

In business, there is really no such thing as an enemy. And that is why Robin held her tongue when leaving her old employer to help Linda start The Kaplan Thaler Group:

One of my former colleagues derided our new agency, saying, "I'll bet they'll crash and burn." The comment made me angry, and the temptation to strike back was strong. But fortunately I didn't do that. The payoff came years later, when I returned to visit my old agency. Some of the firm's most talented employees pulled me aside and said, "Do you have anything for me at your place?"

So I hired them. And now they are tremendous assets to our company. Had I retaliated against my former employer, I would never have had the chance to reunite with my colleagues and enjoy the benefits of their talents.

MAKE FRIENDS—BEFORE THEY CAN BECOME ENEMIES

When Bill Clinton sailed to Oxford to begin his Rhodes scholarship, he shook everybody's hand on the ship. When someone asked him why, he replied that one day he wanted to be the president of the United States—and he was going to need a lot of friends.

Clinton knew that "ya gotta have friends" to get ahead in this world. We all do. So make friends with your adversaries now—before they have a chance to become your enemies.

In the advertising business, clients hire research companies to test the agencies' ads. The research companies have the power to kill the agencies' ideas. The creative people at the agencies often feel that the researchers' advice waters down their ideas and makes them less distinctive. You may be over the top about your brilliant new advertising campaign, only to have a researcher say, "No, I'm sorry, three ladies in New Jersey didn't like your commercial." It's frustrating, and it creates a natural adversarial relationship.

We had a tendency to feel this way as well, until, through our relationship with Aflac, we started working with a man named Gerry Lukeman. Gerry is chairman emeritus of Ipsos-ASI, a company that does a large percentage of the copy testing in the industry. At one point it hit us: *Why are we making him the enemy? He can help us.* So we did something that's very unusual in our business—we asked him to review our storyboards *before* we produced them for test. He gave us great advice, and we went on to create a breakthrough campaign.

When someone challenges or even kills your ideas, you could see him as the enemy—or you could see him as someone who is pushing you to do your best. In the 1950s when Rod Serling wanted to produce a series of television plays about issues like segregation, anti-Semitism, and poverty, the network gave Rod a flat no. So instead Serling disguised his morality plays in the world of science fiction, creating the hit TV show *The Twilight Zone.* His "enemies" at the network actually ended up helping him to create a series that was far better and more popular than a preachy morality show.

That's why in every potential confrontation, your enemy can be the best friend you have.

BRING THE ENEMY OVER TO YOUR SIDE

One of the reasons that the Republican Party has done so well in recent years is that they are extremely good at framing the debate. Most Americans supported the "estate tax," feeling it was something that affected only the very wealthy. But when Republicans successfully got members of the media and the government to start calling it the "death tax," suddenly support for it dropped—hey, we're all going to have *that* experience. Republicans no longer talk about "global warming"—now they just use the innocuous phrase "climate change." People who believe in creationism over evolution are described as favoring "intelligent design."

Whether you agree with the GOP or not, you can take a lesson from their very successful politicking. Don't tell others what you're against—tell them what you're *for*. You can reframe any conversation you have, bringing your opponent over to your side. As Jay Leno told us, "You can say 'Close the damn window,' or you can say 'Is it cold in here?' Asking 'Is it cold in here?' actually works better, because you're then asking a question that people can respond to."

You're also making closing the window the other guy's idea, which we've learned is one of the best ways to get *your* ideas accepted. If we have a client who doesn't like an ad that we think is terrific, we'll ask him what he would do to improve it. If we like his idea, we might say, "I never thought of it that way. Incorporating your idea into the commercial would probably make it a lot better." Once their input has been folded in, they own it—and, of course, are 100 percent behind it.

COME IN PEACE

They are such simple gestures—waving hello, bringing flowers to dinner, clinking glasses. But their origins reveal something very deep about human nature. Each gesture was designed to tell others, "I'm not a threat." Our ancestors would raise their hands and wave hello to show that they were unarmed. People brought gifts to neighbors' homes to demonstrate their good intentions when entering their territory. And beer steins were clinked so that the brew would splash together and everyone would know that no one was getting poisoned.

We're an insecure species. That's why you need to do a little work to help others relax and show that you're a friend. Your body language can speak volumes on this score. There are lots of ways to tell people, "I'm unarmed." Getting up from your desk and sitting next to a visitor to your office is one. Having open body language—arms and legs uncrossed—is another. Tilting your head signals, "I'm interested." Opening both palms tells the other person, "I'm being straight with you."

Another way to learn about honesty and trust is to pay attention to your kids, as Linda and her husband, Fred, learned at the USCF National Scholastic Chess Tournament.

The competition for the first-grade title was down to two boys. One was clearly in the lead. Then he made a punishing mistake: After his move, he forgot to stop his clock. Unless he realized his error, his time would run out and he'd lose the game.

The coaches paced around the room nervously. The audience was stone silent. No one was allowed to tell the young boy about his clock. The only person in the room who was allowed to was his opponent, the other six-year-old sitting across the table, and he was under no obligation to do so. Why should he? If his opponent failed to stop his clock, he would win.

As the clock ticked on, everyone held their breath. Then the other boy leaned over and whispered into the ear of his opponent, who subsequently put his clock down; he went on to win the match.

The boy who lost the match was Linda and Fred's son, Michael:

Afterward, one of the kids asked Michael, "Did you know that if you hadn't said anything you could have won?"

He replied, "I didn't want to win that way. That's not really winning."

We were never prouder of our son than at that moment.

The following week, at an assembly for the entire school that the parents were invited to, the head coach of the chess team told the audience, "I want to honor somebody who is a true champion." And he turned to Michael. Everyone in the auditorium stood up. It was one of the proudest moments of his young life. And, ultimately, he got what he wanted—the pride of being singled out as a winner, of being a role model for the other students.

NICE CUBE

NICE CUBE

Think of the person who irritates you the most. Then try to find something genuinely nice to say about him. Offer this compliment the next time you see him. Repeat with the person who irritates you the second most, third most, and so on.

NICE CUBE

NICE CUBE

List your three fiercest rivals. For each one, write down something that you could do to help them that would not hinder your own business, campaign, et cetera. At the next opportunity, offer your assistance.

NICE CUBE

NICE CUBE

Designate one day a week as completely "gossip free." Do not read trade magazines, the business section of the paper, your favorite insider Web site—anything where you are going to be checking your "score" against someone else's. Gradually work up to two days a week, and so on.

Chapter 6

Tell the Truth

During World War II, General Dwight D. Eisenhower would routinely walk among the troops. One day, as the soldiers were preparing for battle, Eisenhower noticed a young man who seemed silent and depressed.

"How are you feeling, son?" he asked.

"General," he said, "I'm awfully nervous. I was wounded two months ago and just got back from the hospital yesterday. I don't feel so good."

Many generals would have tried to buck up the frightened soldier's spirits, saying, "You don't need to be scared. You've got the best damn army in the world behind you." Instead, Eisenhower said, "Well, you and I are a great pair, then, because I'm nervous too. . . . Maybe if we just walk along together to the river we'll be good for each other."[1]

Eisenhower revealed himself in the most humble way, and that's one of the reasons his troops were so devoted to him. He became a great leader not by being rigid and fearsome, but by being honest and human. "His grin, his mannerisms, his approach to life all exuded sincerity. He wore his heart on his sleeve. There was nothing devious about him. It is perhaps a paradox that it was for this reason that he was an outstanding diplomat, a profession in which the guarded truth and the half-truth are supposed to count for much," historian Stephen Ambrose writes in *The Supreme Commander: The War Years of Dwight D. Eisenhower.*

To us Dwight Eisenhower's success, as a general or a diplomat, is not a paradox at all. To the contrary, we believe honesty is essential to success in any endeavor—whether commanding armies, running a business, organizing a church social, or raising children. Michael S. Gazzaniga, director of the Center of Cognitive Neuroscience at Dartmouth, says that there are certain moral imperatives that all human societies share. "Highest among these," Gazzaniga writes in *The Ethical Brain,* "are that all societies believe that murder and incest are wrong, that children are to be cared for and not abandoned [and] that we should not tell lies or break promises."

Of course, we all know that telling the truth is considered a good thing. Schoolchildren everywhere are taught the story of George Washington and the cherry tree. It's no coincidence that "Thou shalt not lie" is one of the Ten Commandments.

But even as we tell our kids that "honesty is the best policy," many of us believe that we'll go further in life if we can package the truth at times, or even keep it under wraps. We worry about the repercussions of telling someone something they don't want to hear. Because we don't want to hurt other people's feelings, we keep our lips zipped. We find it quicker and easier to tell a white lie at times. We hide our emotions, or try not to let others know how we're feeling or what we're thinking. But the fact is, telling the truth is one of the most direct routes to getting ahead in the world. As Mark Twain once wrote, "The best thing about telling the truth is you never have to think about what to say."

HEAR NO EVIL, SEE NO EVIL

You can't tell the truth if you're not willing to hear it from others. This is particularly important if you're a manager or boss. You have to create an environment where your employees are comfortable telling you that they think your brilliant creative idea is a dud, or that the slightly racy joke you've been telling might offend a buttoned-down client or a fellow employee.

In *Conspiracy of Fools,* author Kurt Eichenwald details a scene where the head of Enron's retail division, Lou Pai, has to explain to Enron president Jeff Skilling why his division will never make a sizable profit, using a slide to illustrate:

> *The story on the slide was the same one Skilling had heard before. Because of high fixed costs, the potential profit margin for the business was low. Pai began explaining the numbers. Skilling didn't want to hear it.*
>
> *"Lou, you're too [expletive deleted] smart for this," he snapped. "I don't want to ever see this slide again."*
>
> *Pai's face was hard. "Jeff, it's the truth."*
>
> *"I just don't want to see that slide ever again."*
>
> *Pai slammed his hand on the table. "It's the [expletive deleted] facts, Jeff!"*
>
> *"It may be the facts," Skilling shouted back. "But I don't want you to think about it that way."*

When Enron executives weren't willing to hear the truth, they sent a message to their employees: Lie. Fudge the numbers, move things around a bit, get creative with the accounting. The trouble is, once you start playing loose with the facts, you're on a slippery slope. You tell one lie, and you have to tell an even bigger lie to cover up the first one. Pretty soon, you're spending all your time and resources trying to manage your lies, rather than building a company. It's an incredible waste of energy and can damage you intellectually and physically. That's why lie-detector machines work. When you lie, your entire physiology changes—your heart rate, your breathing rate, your blood pressure, your perspiration. The polygraph can read your body's natural alarm system going off.

TAKE DOWN YOUR GAME FACE

Ad executive Elizabeth Cogswell Baskin was standing in an elevator with her client at the United Parcel Service headquarters, headed to a meeting. Baskin asked the client how things were going, and the client suddenly burst into tears.

"She told me that every morning her three-year-old son stands outside her shower sobbing because she has to leave for work at 6 A.M. and doesn't come home until 7 or 8 at night. It was tearing her apart," says Baskin, the CEO of Tribe Inc. Advertising in Atlanta.

Many people would have been horrified and embarrassed by such an outburst. After all, in corporate America, crying in the office is one of the biggest taboos. But Baskin didn't shrink away; in fact, she offered the client a job. "We had lunch, and I told her that I'd been thinking about hiring someone who could run my agency and eventually be president. She immediately said, 'I could do that!'" So Baskin offered her the job. "It was the best hire I ever made," she said.

This might seem like a reckless move—after all, Baskin had only had about six or seven meetings with her client. But Baskin had noticed the way she moved around the very stiff, conservative UPS headquarters. "I saw the way she would tap someone on the shoulder. She was very warm and loving, which stood out in that very formal environment."

Warm and loving? This is how you get to be the president of a company? Well, certainly not all companies. In the recent corporate scandals, you can bet that the executives who were frog-marched out of their office doors in handcuffs didn't write "warm and loving" on their résumés. You can bet they never hired someone after a teary outburst.

But Baskin was impressed that her client had the courage to reveal her true feelings. She understood that someone who can show their genuine emotions is an asset to the company. This, of course, is not the conventional wisdom. There's an idea in business that the best way to conduct oneself is to be cold and stone-faced. We recall the boss who, after an important meaning, would lean over victoriously and say, "Well, John really revealed himself in that one." As if our boss had won a big conquest. We also recall a coworker who, after a meeting with a client, crowed, "We really pulled the wool over his eyes."

The problem with such a strategy is that the person who is skilled at hiding his emotions is probably also going to be quite skilled at deception. In the short term, this can work out—they may bluster their way into someone's office and get the job, or win the project from an unsuspecting client. But over time, clients and coworkers will realize this person cannot be trusted. And that's when doors are closed and opportunities missed.

Baskin's respect for emotional honesty is rare in corporate America, but perhaps her approach will catch on as more women assume decision-making roles in the country's biggest companies.

FAKING IT DOESN'T MAKE IT

The first time Larry King ever went on the radio, he says that his mouth felt like it was filled with cotton. He was so nervous that he had to make three attempts before he could speak. When he finally spoke, he recalls in his book *How to Talk to Anyone, Anytime, Anywhere,* he said: "Good morning. This is my first day ever on the radio. I've always wanted to be on the air. I've been practicing all weekend. Fifteen minutes ago they gave me my new name. I've had a theme song ready to play. But my mouth is dry. I'm nervous. And the general manager just kicked open the door and said, 'This is a communications business.'"

This might seem like a strange way to begin a radio career, but King knew that if he leveled with his listeners there was a better chance that they would be on his side. And it worked like a charm.

In business, you often hear the term "fake it till you make it." You're supposed to get in the door with a lot of bluster and bravado—and *then* figure out what the heck you're doing. We think this is terrible advice. As Robin always tells our employees:

Ask me for help when I can still help. I will never criticize an employee who comes to me and says, "I don't know how to do this" or "I feel in over my head." But if someone waits until it's twenty-four hours before the client meeting and then says that they didn't have enough time, then all we can do is cry over it together.

FINE-TUNE YOUR INSTINCTS

On some level, you already know how to sort the honest people from the jerks. Whenever you meet someone new, something deep down inside you says, *He's OK* or *I don't trust that guy.* As Woody Allen once wrote, "There are some people you love, and some people you just want to pinch."

How do we make such snap judgments? We're able to detect nonverbal body signals that tell us whether or not to trust someone. For some people, reading body cues is a professional necessity. Poker players, for example, will tell you that if a person looks down and to the left, they're lying.

We might not all have the skills of a professional poker player, but deep down we all have solid instincts that enable us to detect when someone isn't being straight with us. Harvard psychologist Martha Stout says that because young children don't have fully developed language skills, they're much more reliant on nonverbal cues, like body language and tone of voice. It's for this reason that young children, as well as dogs, are much better than adults at detecting dishonest, and even sociopathic, people.

Surprisingly, even brain-damaged people have this ability—sometimes more so than those of us who are healthy. Author and neurologist Oliver Sacks was very surprised the day he walked by the aphasia ward of his hospital and heard patients howling with laughter. What was so funny? They were listening to a politician giving a speech on television. People with aphasia are unable to understand words, but they are incredibly adept at reading visual cues. So although they couldn't understand the content of the speech, they knew from the politician's facial expressions and the tone of his voice that he was acting—he was lying. The cadences were off, the gestures false. To them, he looked like a buffoon: thus the high comedy.

It turns out that the rest of us can be taught to reconnect with this ability that we lost as children. University of California psychology professor Paul Ekman says even the most skillful liar will have a certain amount of "leakage" on her face—a fleeting expression that suggests she is fibbing. Ekman says that anyone can learn to detect this microexpression—the momentary gap between the words and the emotions—and the training for his lie-detection system has a 95 percent success rate.[2]

Our minds have ways of interpreting things around us separately from our rational brain. If you're trying to decide whether to take that job in Dallas or date the guy you met at your sister's wedding, you can't come to a decision by pure logic, according to author Daniel Goleman. You have to be in touch with your emotions, your gut. It serves as your body's natural alarm system. Usually, gut instincts steer you away from bad decisions—you get a "bad feeling" about a person or a job and decide to keep looking. But our gut can also signal great opportunities.

Unfortunately, many of us are disconnected from our true instincts. We're so inundated with "expert advice" that we've lost the ability to hear our own voices. We can't paint our bathrooms or choose a dinner wine without consulting a barrage of experts, magazine articles, Internet sites, and so on. When conflicts arise with spouses or coworkers, we consult a dozen friends before ever tackling the problem head-on with the other person.

That's why it's so important at times to turn off the computer and listen to your own instincts. They may tell you a lot more than another pumped-up "expert" in the field.

Below are some of the ways we've found to be truthful while not undermining our relationships with others:

START WITH THE GOOD STUFF

At first, Linda was furious:

Two of my creative people had missed several meetings with a client, who became very upset. But before I called the team into my office, I knew I had to deal with my own anger first. I instinctively knew that the best way to resolve the problem wasn't by attacking the people involved head-on, so I waited until I could clear my head before I spoke to them. When I brought them into my office, I began the meeting by telling them some positive truths first. I told them that they needed to understand that they were very important to the client. He looked forward to their meetings, so when they canceled on him it was a very big deal. They responded with surprise—they never realized how much they mattered to the client. Then I went on to explain how valuable their work was on the account. By the end of our conversation, they actually felt empowered. And they haven't missed a meeting since.

If I had let my emotions get the better of me, I would have vented and ranted, and everyone would have left the meeting feeling bad. And it probably wouldn't have done our client any good in the long term. By coming at the problem less confrontationally, however, the team rallied to become far more proactive on the account.

When someone does something wrong, the desire to attack is strangely seductive. You feel that your anger empowers you with the right to retaliate with a heartfelt truth. But the reality is, such anger will get you nowhere. Berating others about how right you are and how wrong they are gets you little. Instead, take a cue from Sergeant Joe Friday—"Just the facts, ma'am." Instead of a personal attack—"What were you thinking? How could you do this?"—just explain matter-of-factly what they did wrong in a way that will help them to accept the truth without feeling demoralized. Then offer a solution—suggesting ways the other person can improve their performance—and move on.

And when you have to deliver difficult news, do it in person. We recently read of an incident where a business traveler was sitting on an airplane that was about to leave the gate. Her cell phone rang. It was her boss—telling her she was fired! As the flight attendants asked the passengers to please turn off all electronic devices, she was being told to come in the next day and clean out her desk. Imagine—just as she was about to put in four or five hours of boring, uncomfortable airplane time she received the ultimate insult, and then had to sit there and think about it in her middle coach seat.

In an age where people break up with lovers via e-mail, taking the time to speak to someone face-to-face when confronting them with a problem is essential. The truth may hurt at times, but it's a lot more humane, and ultimately more appreciated.

HELP THEM TO FIND THE TRUTH THEMSELVES

Let's say your best friend is in a terrible, hurtful relationship. Every other day, she calls you sobbing about what Mr. Wrong did today—criticizing her in front of her boss, neglecting to invite her to his brother's wedding, blowing off her birthday. Her misery is driving you mad; you just want to scream, "Dump the creep, already, would you!"

But as any therapist will tell you, you can't say that. On one level, your friend already knows what she has to do, but she needs to figure it out herself. This same psychology is as true in the workplace with colleagues or clients as it is in your personal relationships. Dr. Gary Belkin, associate professor of psychiatry at NYU Medical School, says that there are ways to push or encourage distraught friends and family members in the right direction. He recalls a patient who was in a relationship that she was ambivalent about and wasn't handling well. When Belkin told her that she seemed to be doing better than she had in her last relationship, the patient pointed out that she still wasn't handling the relationship as well as she could be. Suddenly, changing her behavior became her idea, rather than her psychiatrist saying, "Here's what you need to do."

Whether you are a manager or a business owner, a colleague or a friend, when you're able to help others discover a solution on their own, you're helping them to not just solve the problem but to find a way to solve future problems as well.

FIND THE STRENGTH IN THE WEAKNESS

Several years ago, we hired a very talented account director who had been fired from his last two agencies. As we discovered, the reason was simple: He had a terrible temper. He yelled at his assistants, his partners, even his clients. Soon we had to tell him the bitter truth: That his uncontrollable temper was undermining his career. That unless he enrolled in an anger-management course, he would be fired from this job as well.

We knew this truth would be difficult for him to hear and accept. So we began our meeting by saying that we felt that the reason he gets angry is that he's a perfectionist. He wants to do a stellar job on every project. And it makes him impatient when things go off course.

We weren't excusing his intemperate behavior, but we were showing him that we appreciated the level of care he brings to his work. We were also recognizing that his quick temper was a side effect of his perfectionism, rather than something that defines his entire character.

According to psychologist David Kipper, our weaknesses are often the flip side to our strengths. For example, someone who is extremely focused and good at problem-solving might be very impatient and have a difficult time functioning at a high level in long meetings. A manager who is excellent at seeing the big picture and creating a vision for the company may not fully understand the nitty-gritty of getting things done.

When we spoke to our hotheaded executive, he was shocked at the others' reactions to his behavior. Apparently no one, even his past bosses, had told him how disruptive he was being. He came back the next day and thanked us for giving him the tough love he needed to help see, and change, his behavior. He was completely willing to work on his anger problem, because he didn't want to lose his job and he understood that we recognized something very positive about the source of his anger and impatience—his perfectionism.

Today, while he still struggles with this tendency to be hot tempered, he has come a long way in restraining his behavior and being more respectful of others. And we, in turn, have recognized his improvement by having him work on more high-profile pitches and accounts, as well as having him tackle more complex projects that require a lot of attention to detail—tasks that others might not have had the patience for. As a result, he is now at the top of his profession and has helped the agency land several multi-million-dollar accounts.

THE TRUTH DOESN'T ALWAYS HURT

Robin agonized for a week after her college-age daughter asked if she could move in with her boyfriend, in an apartment that her parents would pay for:

I felt that Melissa was too young to make such a big life choice. Moving in with a boyfriend is really a declaration of one's independ-

ence, not something that should be subsidized by one's parents. Plus, an apartment in New York would be even more expensive than the New York University dorm that Melissa lived in.

So even though I knew the answer from minute one, I spent a week stressing over what to say, asking everyone I knew for an opinion. Melissa is twenty years old, so I needed to respond to her as an adult. I couldn't just act like a mother, saying, "No, because I said so" as if she were ten years old. It required finding a way to talk about her feelings and have an adult conversation. It was a therapist who gave me the $185 question: "How did you get to that, Melissa?"

It turns out, Melissa reminded me, that I had mentioned once that I thought that buying an apartment for her might be a good investment. When I asked what would happen if I didn't want to do that anymore, she said, "I'd live in the dorm."

End of drama. We often think that in order to resolve a conflict all parties must agree. But that isn't true. At the end of a discussion, you don't have to agree, you just need to feel that each of you has been heard, says Harvard negotiation teacher Sheila Heen. When you listen and ask questions, you give the other person some control and show that you respect their point of view. And you've created a situation where the other person can hear your perspective, rather than your attempting to shut them down with a "No!"

Confronting one's child may be painful at times, but ultimately that's a parent's right. What's much harder is confronting a client. We certainly don't advise doing this on a regular basis, but as Maurice Lévy, our friend and the CEO of our parent company, the Publicis Groupe, discovered, sometimes you have to tell an important client something they don't want to hear.

For years, Maurice was frustrated with a very finicky client. Each year, the client would systematically ask to change the leader of the team or even the whole team. For several years, the request was granted, even when it was unjustified. Finally, Maurice had had enough. When the client asked him to get rid of one of his most talented managers, Maurice refused, explaining that this woman was the best person for the job and that he could not let the client abuse the agency's people.

The client was furious, threatening to pull the account if Maurice didn't honor his wishes, but Maurice wouldn't budge. A few days passed and nothing happened. He kept his account with the agency and the team was kept intact. "We understand the necessity to make some important changes when it is justified, but when a client abuses this understanding, it places us in a lose-lose situation: against the agency and its teams, and against the client, because no team would be comfortable giving the best of themselves," says Maurice.

Twenty years went by, and few people knew how Maurice had risked his career to stick up for one of his people. But when the manager retired, she told the story at a small good-bye gathering at the office. Her coworkers were astonished to learn how much the agency had stuck up for her—and word of this loyalty quickly spread throughout the company.

The real strength of Maurice's decision to call the client's bluff was not about what happened then, but the fact that this act reverberated with the company twenty years later. Imagine how inspired those employees must have felt when they learned that they had a boss who would put so much on the line for them.

DON'T BE AFRAID TO SET BOUNDARIES

Years ago, Linda told an editor that she needed to begin work on a particular project at 8 A.M. the next Monday:

He said it was impossible for him. So we moved the meeting to 10, and the work got done.

Afterward I asked him, "I'm just curious—what other appointment did you have at 8 on Monday morning?"

"I didn't have an appointment. That's the time that I spend with my kids."

"What did you mean when you said meeting at 8:00 was 'impossible'?"

"It's impossible. That's not the way I operate my life."

He taught me a lesson that day. We are all entitled to steer our own ships; we all have the right to establish boundaries. It is OK to tell someone that you have "other plans" if they suggest something that doesn't work for you. And those plans don't have to involve meeting the Queen or serving as the best man in a wedding.

We've all had those moments when we scramble for an excuse to get out of something we don't want to do. You receive an invitation to an acquaintance's bridal shower and just don't have the time. Your boss asks if you could come in for a Saturday meeting on something you could have done during the week. An old college friend calls out of nowhere and asks if you would like to attend her open-mike poetry reading tonight.

Out come a torrent of pained regrets: "Sorry! I'm visiting the gravesite of my great-aunt Millie this weekend!" "Gee, I'd love to, but I'm having a double root canal!" If that's you, stop. You don't *need* to offer a list of reasons why you can't get together or fashion your schedule around someone else's. You don't need to spin a sob story or fake a prior commitment just so you can spend your weekend with your family. There's no need to elaborate. Simply respond. As therapist Dr. Ona Robinson says, "Never explain, never defend, never justify." You have a right to live your life and set your own boundaries. And others will respect you all the more for doing so.

If you're open to getting together, but at a time that fits your own schedule, offer the other person an alternative—suggest another time to meet, or initiate an invitation to them the next time.

NICE CUBE: GO ON A TRUTH DIET

For one week, try telling nothing but the truth to everyone you talk with. You don't have to go out of your way to tell a coworker that you think her earrings are hideous. But don't tell her "They're beautiful!" if you don't mean it. Try "They're interesting! Where did you get them?" If you don't want to attend your second cousin's baby shower, send her a simple note apologizing and saying you won't be able to make it. Just tell her how happy you are for her, and send a nice gift.

NICE CUBE

NICE CUBE: THE COURAGE TO BE HONEST

Is there something that you're refraining from saying to someone because you fear that the truth would hurt their feelings? Ask yourself: Would they be better off knowing the truth? If the answer is yes, then tell them, but find a way to do it gently. If the problem is your sister's unrealistic career expectations, wait until the next time she is complaining about her dead-end job and then ask her what she wants out of a job, what she's doing to get the kind of job she would like, and so on. Guide her to see the truth for herself, rather than slamming her in the face with it. For example, "I admire your ambition, but do you think that the leap from bank teller to hedge-fund manager is realistic? What about being a hedge-fund manager attracts you, besides the money? . . ."

NICE CUBE

NICE CUBE: TAKE OFF YOUR MASK

In situations where we feel vulnerable, it's easiest to just keep our game face firmly fixed. If you're used to hiding behind a mask, try lifting it . . . gradually. Think of something you don't like revealing to others: that you stole a book from the library as a child, or that you're afraid to cold-call a potential date for fear of being rejected. Then find three people you trust and tell them. The point is not to go around telling your boss or your future in-laws about all your failures and frailties, but to find people you trust with whom you can be open and vulnerable. Ultimately, you'll find that you really don't need to walk around pretending to be someone else—because who you are is just fine.

NICE CUBE

NICE CUBE: PLAY "AND THEN WHAT WILL HAPPEN?"

Being honest and forthright can sound great in theory, but what about situations where you have to tell an uncomfortable truth? Robin had a boss who asked his employees to do this exercise. The next time you're worried that someone is going to be upset at your honesty, imagine that you're right: You tell them the truth and they hate you for it. What will happen? Will you lose the account? Lose your job? Will your wife or husband walk out on you? Will you have to sell your home? Will you be sentenced to death? We didn't think so. By imagining how bad the consequences could be, you'll usually find they are not that bad—thereby putting your own fears into perspective.

Chapter 7

"Yes" Your Way to the Top

When Lupe Valdez ran for sheriff of Dallas County, nobody thought she could win. "I started this campaign with five strikes against me: I'm a woman, I'm Hispanic, I'm a lesbian, I was an outsider to the sheriff's department, and I'm a Democrat," says Valdez. Her opponent was a Republican man who had worked at the Dallas sheriff's department for thirty years.

In the final days of the race, Valdez's opponent started a vicious negative campaign, falsely accusing her of inappropriately taking money from a gay-rights organization. Valdez's underfunded campaign chose not to respond in another negative manner. "There was tremendous pressure on me from my staff to answer back with a negative response. We knew we couldn't just let the accusations stand without doing something, so I decided to take a different route. That way, if I lost, I would still like who I am,'" says Valdez.

Valdez and her staff took the positive step of calling

60,000 female voters who did not vote a straight party ticket in the previous election. Valdez felt that if she could get her message out to these women, she could convince them to vote for her—without stooping to her opponent's tactics. The election came, and in a county where a sheriff's election has never been won by more than 300 votes, Valdez won by 17,000 votes and is now the first woman ever elected sheriff of Dallas County.

Most people give lip service to the idea of "staying positive," but when an opponent attacks, the usual response is to take the gloves off. After all, what are the choices? Stand up and fight, or sit down and take it.

But Valdez found a third strategy that was both strong *and* nice. Instead of dragging down the esteem of both candidates in the minds of voters, she recruited more voters. Instead of saying "no" to her opponent and his backers, she found a way to say "yes" to the women of Dallas County.

As Valdez learned, "yes" is the most powerful word in the English language. If you can learn to say "yes" to every client, boss, and new business prospect, you'll be able to skip climbing up the corporate ladder and take the express elevator instead.

That's because being positive has a huge impact on all of your relationships, as psychologist John Gottman found. Gottman videotaped 700 couples shortly before they wedded. After watching each fifteen-minute recording, the team predicted which couples they thought would stay together and which would divorce. Ten years later, they found that they predicted the marriage success rates *with 94 percent accuracy.*

The researchers were able to make such stunningly accurate predictions by monitoring interactions that most of us might find inconsequential—a reassuring arm squeeze, a frustrated eye roll. They discovered that the negative interactions have a very detrimental impact on a marriage. In fact, it took five positive exchanges—smiles, jokes, compliments—to make up for one negative one.

Research on workplace interactions has yielded similar results. In one study, employees were much more productive when the ratio of positive to negative exchanges was at least three to one.[1]

"No" shuts down possibilities, while "yes" opens them up. Bob realized this after he interviewed a very unlikely candidate for a sales job. The man who walked into his office, John, was four feet tall. He had no knees and no hands, and his arms stopped at the elbow. "When I first saw him I thought, 'Whoa.' But after talking to him for five minutes, I realized I had completely forgotten that there was anything different about him. And he seemed like a great salesman," says Bob.

John had been trying to get a sales job for months. He'd interviewed at more than one hundred different offices, but no one would hire him. "He said, 'I know I can do it. Just give me a chance,'" said Bob.

Bob was convinced, but his bosses were worried. Would he make the clients uncomfortable? What if he demanded a lot of expensive elevators or other special equipment? What if they had to let him go and he sued them for discrimination?

There were a lot of unknown variables to John, and it would have been easier to just say no. Finally, Bob convinced his bosses to say "yes" to John. The risk paid off handsomely: John turned out to be one of the best salesmen the company ever had. His hard work, engaging personality, and laser-sharp intelligence were ultimately what won over the clients. And John says that in some ways unusual looks turned out to be an advantage. "I don't remember every person I meet, but every person I meet remembers *me*!" says John.

How can you bring a memorable "yes" to every encounter you have?

ASSUME YES

When therapist Ona Robinson begins working with couples, she often starts with a homework assignment: Name three reasons why cannibalism is good. She gets a lot of hilarious responses—"excellent source of protein," "not too much fat," "reduces world population," "all-natural ingredients."

The point of the exercise is not to defend cannibalism but to help people develop the habit of assuming goodwill. When you approach others with the assumption that they have generous intentions, you'll find that your life becomes a much easier ride.

For example, say someone tells you that they hate what you're wearing. You could say something nasty back, or you could thank them for being concerned about your appearance. The actual intention of the person doing the clothing critique is unimportant. What matters is that you train yourself to interpret the encounter in a positive way.

Research conducted by psychologist Martin Seligman confirms the benefits of optimism. In a study of insurance salesmen, Seligman found that pessimists are more realistic than optimists, but that optimists are more successful.

The reason has to do with the way optimists talk to themselves. When an optimist is rejected on a sales call, she tells herself that the person was probably too busy or in a bad mood. It's a temporary condition that says nothing about the insurance agent's skill—she just had the bad luck to call at the wrong time. Or she won't think about the reason at all—she'll move on to the next call.

When a pessimist faces rejection, her self-dialogue is very different. She'll find a permanent and pervasive reason why the rejection happened. She'll tell herself that she's a bad salesman, that she'll never make it in this business. The pessimist gets demoralized and makes few calls—and thus has fewer sales.

It's just as Henry Ford said: "If you think you can't, you're right. And if you think you can, you're right."[2]

When you treat people like idiots, they will often meet your expectations. But if you treat them like the smartest, most talented people in the world, you'll be amazed by what they accomplish. In the end, being a cheerleader is far more effective than being a drill sergeant.

EXPRESS THE YES

As we mentioned earlier, researchers have found that only 7 percent of our communication is verbal—the other 93 percent of expression comes from body language, facial expressions, and tone of voice.[3] That's why it's not enough to *say* "yes"; you have to *express the yes.*

One of the best ways to do this is to simply nod. Allan

Pease, a consultant who has taught body-language skills and techniques to businesspeople for thirty years, says that nodding is one of the most universal human gestures—even people who have been blind since birth nod their head to say "yes." Another universal gesture is tilting the head to the side to show interest. In fact, Charles Darwin noted that even animals share this habit. "When others are speaking to you, all you need to do is use the head-tilted position and head nods to make the other person feel warm towards you," Pease writes in his book *Signals*.

In fact, in a well-known experiment, a psychology class decided to test this theory using their professor as the guinea pig.[4] Without the teacher's knowledge, every time he walked to the right side of the classroom, the students would become distracted and inattentive. But every time he walked to the left side of the room, they would look up, smile, and give him approving nods. Can you guess what happened? The professor ended up teaching the entire class leaning against the left wall of the room! This is the power of a nonverbal acknowledgment.

Mirroring is another great tool, one that therapists use all the time. The next time you have an important meeting with a prospective client or employer, reflect their gestures back to them subtly. For example, if she picks up a coffee cup with her right hand, pick up a pencil with your left hand. Don't mimic her gestures exactly—that will just look weird. Just attune yourself to her posture and her mood, and you'll be quietly communicating that you accept her and are receptive to her ideas—and that, in turn, will put her at ease and of course make her more open to your brilliant proposals!

GET OFF THE "NO" TRAIN

The problem with the word "no" is that it sets off a chain of negative events. If you receive withering criticism from your boss, you're going to have a bad feeling about it. And even if you can't express that feeling at the moment, it's going to come out eventually. You might decide to start coming in late, which annoys the coworker who has to cover for you. She subsequently decides, "No, I can't take over for you while you're away on vacation." You begin a chain of "no"s that's hard to stop.

Improv performers understand this. If you've ever watched really great improvisational theater, you know that it's an amazing experience. The actors are given a completely random suggestion—alligators, outer space, mincemeat—and create a story on the spot, without ever taking a minute to consult each other or even think about what they want to say. When it's done well, the results are usually hilarious—and much more entertaining than the most well-rehearsed performance.

While watching, you might wonder how the actors could possibly create such clever, witty stories off the top of their heads. Talent certainly accounts for a lot, but it's not just that. There are many tricks that improv performers use to keep the narrative flowing, and one of the most important rules is that improv performers never, ever say no. The response must always be "Yes, and . . ."

For example, say one performer begins by gazing into his partner's eyes and saying, "Let's get married on Mars."

If the other performer says, "What, are you crazy! Mars

is a zillion degrees and has no oxygen," where do you think the skit will go? Nowhere fast.

On the other hand, if the performer says, "Yes, that would be wonderful. We'll invite all my cousins from Neptune and Pluto," then you've got a story.

Granted, it's not easy to say yes all the time. A woman we know named Bonnie recalls a rainy weekend when, exhausted from months of fruitless house hunting in New York City, she planned to stay home with a good book. Then her friend Terry called to invite her to a picnic in New Jersey, hosted by his friend George. "You can imagine how enthused I was about going to Jersey in the rain for a barbecue," says Bonnie.

She had met George only once—when Terry brought him to a party that she had hosted. But Terry explained that George was a firm believer in reciprocity and wanted very much to repay Bonnie for her hospitality. "It's just how he was raised," says Bonnie.

So Bonnie went to the bus station with her book in hand, ready for a long, tedious journey. Instead, she found herself at her destination ten minutes after departing the station. "I was pleasantly surprised to have a magnificent view of Manhattan," she says. She also noticed many beautiful restored Victorian houses in the area. When she got to the barbecue, she inquired about the prices of the homes in the area. George mentioned that a house was for sale across the street, but the asking price was out of her price range. Nevertheless, Bonnie had a great time at the barbecue and the next day sent George a thank-you gift.

Two weeks later, Bonnie got a call from George, who had negotiated the price of the house down into her range. "He convinced the owners that if they didn't use a real estate agent this would work out well for them," says Bonnie.

It was a dream house for Bonnie and her husband, and they purchased it. "We're ten minutes from the city, and my husband is five minutes from fishing. Best of all, we have the nicest neighbor we could hope for. Who would have thought that the light at the end of the tunnel for a die-hard New Yorker would be New Jersey?"

FOUR WAYS TO SAY "YES" INSTEAD OF "NO"

But you can't possibly say yes to everyone all the time. Sometimes the answer really is no. As in "No, you can't go on spring break with twelve other sixteen-year-olds." "No, I can't come in to work for the fifth weekend in a row."

You also might feel that saying yes has never been very difficult for you. You say yes to *everyone*—your coworkers, your mother-in-law, the Daisy Scouts—and it's killing you!

"Yes-ing your way to the top" does not mean doing everyone else's bidding. It simply means finding *something* to say yes to. So the next time you're tempted to say no, try one of these statements instead:

"YES, I WANT TO HELP."

Recently, Robin received a tip on a new piece of business:

An executive recruiter whom we frequently hire account managers from sent me a referral for some business for the Orthodox Union, an orthodox Jewish group. We couldn't take the job because we already did work for the United Jewish Communities. But I didn't want to just say no, so I called around and found a few friends of the agency who were interested in the account. I ended up spending a bit of time doing this, but it was important to me to help the recruiter. It's a very competitive market out there, and I want her to send us the best people. What better way to show her that this is a nice place to work?

Even if you have to say no personally, there is usually an alternative yes. By helping to solve someone's problem—say, by referring them to someone who might be able to help them—you keep the positive energy in motion. And very often, a request that doesn't sound very attractive to you might be a great opportunity for someone else. The junior associate might be thrilled at the chance to represent the company at the sales conference in Topeka. By setting that up, you're making two people happy—and you've saved yourself an airline ticket.

"YES, YOU CAN DO BETTER."

As mothers and bosses, we very often have to tell people things they don't want to hear. If someone at our office presents work that we don't think is on target, obviously we can't say it's wonderful. But we will try to find something positive to say, something that's true. For example, if a writer brings us a bad script, we remind ourselves that it's just one script—and that he's done many great ones for us. So rather than say, "This is terrible," it's a lot more motivating to say, "You do such terrific work. I'm not sure this is up to your caliber."

"YES, I SEE YOU."

It only takes a minute to send a thank-you note or respond to an unsolicited résumé, but these small acknowledgments are easy to neglect. After all, you have 800,000 things to do. Why take that time if you don't even have a job to offer? But when you toss a résumé in the trash without a response, you're denying someone's existence. That's why we have a policy of responding to every single e-mail and phone call we receive, even if all we say is "I'm afraid we don't have any openings here, but thanks for thinking of us and best of luck."

A simple acknowledgment like this helps build goodwill that can reverberate for decades. The word gets out that your company has nice people—publicity that you really can't buy. And it takes seconds.

If you still think you're too busy to answer all your e-mails, ask yourself if you're busier than the average corporate CEO. A recent *Wall Street Journal* poll found that thirty-nine out of forty-four surveyed CEOs personally answered e-mails from employees—even if it meant replying at 11 P.M. or while standing in an elevator with their BlackBerry. For Dell Computers CEO Michael Dell, that means spending several hours a day reading each one of the roughly 200 e-mails that fall into his in-box in a twenty-four-hour period.

Many of the most powerful people in this country understand the importance of this kind of acknowledgment. New York mayor Michael Bloomberg surprised one disgruntled New Yorker when he answered his home phone at 10 P.M. When reporters asked how the woman got his number, he said it was listed. He told the woman that he didn't mind her calling, but next time he asked that she didn't phone so late.

Are you really busier than Michael Bloomberg or Michael Dell? Take the time to say "yes" to everyone you meet.

"YES, YOUR TALENTS LIE ELSEWHERE."

Warren Buffet says that's he's never fired anyone. He has just helped them to find the right job at his company. We have tried to abide by this philosophy at The Kaplan Thaler Group. If someone is not working out in a particular position, we will keep trying out different positions until we find the right job. We've found that the loyalty that we show our employees comes back many times over.

Unfortunately, we haven't been able to keep a perfect zero-percent firing rate. And no matter how you sugarcoat it, firing somebody is a very big no.

We recently had to fire someone who wasn't interested in switching positions in the company. She was interested in only one job, but she wasn't working out in that position. Even though we let her go, she appreciated the fact that we tried to find a way for her to stay, and she sent a very sweet note saying so. Robin wrote back, "I wish you tremendous luck. I know that there are some great talents within you, and if there's anything I can do to help you discover them, let me know."

Granted, a firing is a firing. It's a terrible, stressful experience that no one chooses. But the truth is, it's often just the push some of us need to get started in the right direction. In graduate school, Linda had just this experience with a music professor:

I studied composition with a Pulitzer Prize–winning composer named Mario Davidovsky, a pioneer in electronic music. I was awful. He wanted me to compose atonal, contemporary music, but everything I wrote sounded like a Broadway ditty. So one day, he looked me straight in the eye and in his thick Argentinean accent said, "Leenda, you cannot do this. But, you will be bery, bery good at writing jingle."

I was crushed. At the time I said, "What an audacious thing to say. What a rude remark." And then, upon later reflection, I realized, "What a great career move." He was 100 percent right, and soon after I began my career in advertising.

Years later, I wrote, "I don't want to grow up, I'm a Toys 'R' Us kid," which is one of the longest-running jingles in American history. I feel extremely grateful to my professor, because he told me, in the nicest way possible, what I couldn't do. And helped me find what I could.

Finally, there are times when saying "no" is simply not an option. Notre Dame football coach Charlie Weis confronted this when a dying boy made a last request: He wanted to call the first play of the next game—"pass right." Unfortunately, the boy passed away before the day of the game, but Weis was determined to fulfill his request. When the game began, it seemed as if the boy's play would not work. The quarterback asked Weis what to do, and he said they had no choice—they would follow the boy's instructions. Not only did the quarterback complete the pass—they made a thirteen-yard gain.

The smart money would have called a different play, of course. But the bottom line is that we really never know what will happen when we say "yes" instead of "no." And sometimes making the "smart" choice is not always the right decision. Sometimes you just have to shut up and listen.

NICE CUBE

NICE CUBE: BECOME AN ACTIVE AUDIENCE

President Clinton was known for his ability to establish an immediate connection with every single person he met. No matter how many people were in the receiving line, he made each person feel like they were the only one in the room, like they were the center of the universe. Contrast that with your last conversation with a vapid social climber at a party—you know, the one who was clearly looking over her shoulder for someone more important to meet and greet.

We all have the ability to make people feel like the most important person in the world. We just have to give them our complete attention and to see ourselves in their eyes. For all the time we spend obsessing in the mirror—about our hair, our thighs, our wrinkles—it's amazing how little time many Americans spend thinking about how they really look to others. The next time you attend a lecture or a large meeting, take a look at the people around you. How many are focused on the speaker? The best way to say "yes" is to simply pay attention.

NICE CUBE

NICE CUBE: FIND THE "YES" IN THE "NO"

Write down the last five things you said no to—the vacation days that an employee wanted, the expensive toy your child asked for, the monster movie your boyfriend wanted to watch. Then ask yourself the following: Was this no absolutely necessary? (The rest of the staff would have been shorthanded for a couple of days, but they also would have seen that you're committed to letting people take time off when they need it.) Was there an alternative yes? (Like suggesting the child do extra chores to earn money to save for the toy.) Could saying yes have benefited you in any way? (Maybe you would have *liked* the monster movie.) Getting in the habit of at least considering "yes" will help end the "chain of nos."

Chapter 8

Shut Up and Listen

Shortly after we started The Kaplan Thaler Group, we had lunch with the CEO of a rival agency, who is now retired. He was very anxious to tell us how superior his company was to ours. We could have argued with him and tried to top his claims, but instead we let him talk. As he waxed on about how brilliant his company was, we quietly listened.

In time, he began disclosing rather intimate details of his company, including his competitive tactics, client fees, agency strategies, and so on. He also mentioned some new business that his company was pursuing, something we weren't invited to pitch. We made the call, got into the pitch, and won the business. Listening, rather than crowing about our own achievements, paid for that lunch many times over.

Why do most of us like to talk so much? Because we want to be noticed. We get a charge out of being the center of the universe. But when you yap on, you use up all of the oxygen and energy in the room, which is debilitating for everyone else.

Moreover, you waste your time. After all, you already know what you know. Every minute you spend trying to wow someone else is a minute you're not getting new information. As Larry King writes, "My first rule of conversation is this: I never learn a thing while I'm talking."

Here's how to fine-tune your listening skills.

LET THE OTHER GUY BE SMARTER

Sometimes it's important to let the world know how smart you are—say, when you're trying to get into Harvard or applying to med school. But the truly intelligent understand the limits of brainpower. According to *Emotional Intelligence*, IQ accounts for only a small percentage of a person's success in life. That's because your IQ, along with most other academic test scores, measures how well you solve problems when you're alone. It can't measure your ability to negotiate a deal, give constructive criticism, or console a friend. This social intelligence will have far more impact on your life than your knowledge of Shakespearean sonnets or mathematical algorithms.

When you let the other guy's brilliance shine through, you not only gain new information, you also earn their goodwill. Everyone likes to be around people who make them feel intelligent. For Jay Leno, this is an ironclad rule of being a talk-show host: "The trick is to make the guest look good at the expense of the host. The shows that tend to fail are the ones where the host looks good at the expense of the guest. Eventually that host realizes, 'Hey, how come I'm not getting these guests anymore?'"

KEEP IT SIMPLE

The Kaplan Thaler Group is very noisy. That's what makes it a fun place to work—there are a lot of Type A people who are very excited to tell everyone their ideas. One day, we were brainstorming about a pitch to Foxwoods, the Connecticut casino. Everyone was throwing out some very high-minded ideas about what made the casino goer tick. We pored over very extended demographic surveys and research. We pondered the casino's intellectual property. We asked such fundamentals as: "What is the essential experience that people look for when they go to a casino?" "What is the real feeling of winning?"

All the while, Chris Wauton, our director of strategic planning, remained quiet. Now Chris is a brilliant, Oxford-educated advertising professional. Of course, to be entirely fair, we've found that anything you say in a British accent automatically sounds 25 percent more intelligent.

Chris had done extensive research at Foxwoods, interviewing numerous customers. When he finally began to speak, we all leaned forward, eager to hear what he had to say. He looked at us and shrugged. "I don't know. It just seems like Foxwoods is, well, *fun*."

We broke out laughing. Of course, he was right. Sometimes the simplest answer is the best one. Chris was able to sum up the experience of going to Foxwoods in a single word, because he had been listening rather than pontificating. And, using his insight in our pitch, we won the business.

ASK, DON'T TELL

Robin learned this lesson early on:

When I first began my advertising career, we had a client, Heublein Distillers, in Connecticut, which was also where our boss lived. Since the boss's house was on the way, I used to pick him up on the days we were meeting with the client. As a result, every day, the most junior person on the team—me—spent an hour each way with one of the most senior persons in the company. I was a little shy about what I'd talk about. He was a big boss, and I didn't want to say anything stupid in front of him.

Over time, I realized that our boss was a great raconteur. He could talk about any subject, however arcane, for hours. So every morning, I would start out asking him a question. For example, I'd ask what he thought about advertising distilled spirits like Smirnoff, our client's No. 1 vodka brand, on television. Or sometimes I'd ask his take on office politics at the agency. And because I was a nobody at the time, he'd tell me everything. I got a ton of inside information, as well as a business school's worth of insight and analysis, just by asking questions and listening.

When you ask questions, you tell people that you care about them, that you're interested in what they have to say. You also send an oh-so-subtle message that you're a bright, inquisitive individual who would like to know more. That's why even the smallest question can have a huge impact. . . .

Ruth Downing Karp began her advertising career at J. Walter Thompson in the days when women wore gloves and hats to work. When she was twenty, she went to her first meeting, in which a researcher made a presentation of various sales statistics that he had analyzed. As he spoke, people in the room peppered him with questions and comments, and at one point Ruth realized she was the only person who hadn't spoken. She was nervous that her silence would make her look like she was uninterested or just wasn't paying attention. So she listened carefully as the researcher said that if they enacted a particular plan the sales growth would be 7½ percent.

Ruth looked up and quietly asked, "Seven and a half percent?"

The researcher looked at her, slightly flustered. "Isn't it seven and a half percent?" he asked. He assumed that she was questioning him because she knew something that he didn't.

"I don't know," she said honestly. "I'm just asking."

Then someone else said, "I see her point. Because when you look at it from a different perspective, it's really not that."

By being quiet, Ruth learned a lot about how to make an intelligent impression. In fact, when the researcher went back over his numbers, he realized he actually did make a mistake! As the Bible says, "Even a fool, when he holdeth his peace, is counted wise." Ruth went on to become one of the top creative directors at the agency.

DON'T ARGUE SO MUCH

You're late for the meeting. You failed to file the report on time. You were going sixty in a forty-miles-per-hour zone. And out come a torrent of long-winded explanations about traffic, communication mishaps, broken speedometers.

Whenever problems or conflicts arise, there is a natural

tendency to try and "talk your way out of it." But sometimes you win your case by shutting up and listening your way out of it.

That's what Jonathan discovered when he was speeding to a wedding that he was late for, with his wife and mother-in-law in tow.

When a police officer pulled him over and informed him that he had been speeding behind an off-duty cop, Jonathan cheerfully said he had no idea. "I joked around with the cop a bit, saying the women made me do it, et cetera. But I didn't argue. What could I do? I was speeding," says Jonathan.

After handing Jonathan the ticket, the cop said very pointedly that sometimes you could fight tickets. Although Jonathan pressed him for details, the officer said he couldn't say any more. So even though the courthouse was two hours away from his hometown, Jonathan decided to go. "I was basically hoping the police officer wouldn't show up so it would be dismissed," says Jonathan.

No such luck. "I get to the courthouse and they say, 'Oh look—it's the guy who speeds behind cops.'"

This was in a small farm town. The judge was wearing a cardigan sweater and jeans. The police officer said, "Judge, when you pull someone over and give them a speeding ticket, how often do you think they are nice to you?"

The judge said, "I don't imagine it would be very often."

The cop thought about it a bit. "Well, you know," he said with a smile, "he was *parked* when I pulled him over."

And with that, Jonathan was left with just a parking ticket and a warning.

EVERYONE IS WORTH A LISTEN

Jay Leno says that when he wants to know if something is funny, he'll ask the least important person in the room. "And I generally use their input. We live in a society of exclusion. There is this idea that you should try to keep people out—'Oh, you can't come into this club, you have to be a member, you don't have enough money, you're not handsome enough.' But if you go through life with the opposite attitude and try to include everybody, it opens up doors."

It can also do great things for your business. We once spoke with the head of a major restaurant chain, who needed to figure out why thousands of the company's plates were broken every year. No one at the executive level could understand what was happening, and it was costing the company a fortune to replace the plates.

One night, the executive discussed this problem with a colleague while dining in one of the chain's restaurants. A waiter overheard this conversation and took him back into the kitchen. He introduced him to one of the kitchen staff. In broken English, a kitchen helper pointed out that the dishwasher in the restaurant had a faulty mechanism in the box, which was causing extreme shaking while the dishes were being washed. The shaking put pressure on the plates, causing them to become brittle and break.

With this knowledge, the restaurant was able to fix the problem and save the chain a huge amount of money. The executive rewarded the employee by giving him a check for $50,000—10 percent of the half million he estimated that the company would save. Furthermore, the executive decreed that every employee who saved the company money by pointing out ways to improve operations would garner 10 percent of the savings.

Abraham Lincoln understood the importance of getting information straight from the source, rather than relying on advisers to interpret the will of the people. In *Lincoln on Leadership,* author Donald T. Phillips describes how Lincoln was one of the first American leaders to understand the importance of circulating. He allowed many citizens to visit him and share their thoughts. "I call these receptions my 'public opinion baths' . . . though they may not be pleasant in all particulars, the effect, as a whole, is renovating and invigorating," Lincoln said. One hundred years later, business gurus Tom Peters and Robert Waterman would call this "Management by Wandering Around."

In trying to understand the average American consumer better, Procter & Gamble vice chairman Susan Arnold took the "Management by Wandering Around" formula one step further. At P&G, there's a saying, "The consumer is boss." Staffers are expected to know the consumer. So for two weeks, Arnold gave herself a budget, after fixed expenses, of $60 a week. This meant she had to grapple with questions like "Do I fill the gas tank or buy shampoo?" She found herself squeezing the last spec of toothpaste out of the tube, and she stopped using parking garages. "I did this along with my entire P&G Beauty Leadership team at the time, about a dozen or so people. The concept was to stay in touch with our consumer by living on the average discretionary income of the consumer in each of our regions," Arnold told us. The key learning from this hands-on study: The women who bought their products were constantly weighing one choice against another. "It is continually about choices—should I spend on the higher-priced shampoo and skip the new lipstick shade, or will the lower-priced shampoo suffice and then I can get the lipstick also? For us, it means that we have to be providing good value to our consumers—the benefits that the product delivers must live up to their price."

Arnold understands what all great leaders know—in business, the more you can empathize with the consumer, the better you can serve them. In fact, empathy has been found to be *the most important* skill for success in life. In the next chapter, we'll tell you why.

NICE CUBE

NICE CUBE: ZIP YOUR LIP

For one day, try to say as little as possible. Try to keep the focus away from yourself. Where you're tempted to tell a story, ask a question. Where you're tempted to say, "Oh, that same thing happened to me . . . ," ask, "How did that make you feel?" Don't be obnoxious about it. If someone asks how you feel about the new sports stadium the city is building, answer the question. But then bring the conversation back to the other person's opinion. At the end of the day, make a list of everything that you learned. How much would you have missed if you had spent the time talking about yourself?

NICE CUBE

NICE CUBE: HONOR YOUR DEBTS

Think you're smart? Finish the following sentences:

"I never would have made it to where I am without . . ."

"I owe a great debt to . . ."

"I take courage from . . ."

"My greatest teacher was . . ."

After all, none of us gets ahead on our own.

Chapter 9

Put Your Head on Their Shoulders

When award-winning journalist and *New Yorker* columnist Ken Auletta was covering the Microsoft antitrust trial for *The New Yorker* magazine and for his book *World War 3.0: Microsoft and Its Enemies,* he scheduled the first of what turned out to be three long interviews with the presiding judge, Thomas Penfield Jackson. Auletta had many hard-hitting questions for Jackson about the trial, Bill Gates, and the judge's many rulings. But the first time they met, Auletta didn't talk about any of those things. "Instead, I asked him about his life and his parents and the formative experiences he had had," says Auletta.

Auletta's approach might seem strange. He was writing a big story for a prestigious magazine and for Random House. Why would he waste his first meeting chitchatting like someone at an ice-cream social? First, he got crucial background information about the judge's values that would give his story depth and context. Second, he got to know the judge better, and the judge got to know him. "I think I gained his trust for not displaying a hunger for a quick headline," says Auletta. "You get much more information by being polite and patient."

Journalists, Auletta points out, don't have a reputation for being nice. Much of the job involves asking very harsh questions: "Did your organization wiretap American citizens?" "Why did you sell your company's stock while telling your employees to buy more?" "How did you feel when your husband ran off with Angelina Jolie?" Sometimes the answers to these questions serve the public interest; other times they just sell copies of gossip magazines. Either way, in order to uncover the cold, hard facts the smart reporter quickly learns to be very, very nice.

"We don't have subpoena power, so people don't have to talk to us," says Auletta. "And they won't talk to us if the experience is like getting their teeth drilled at the dentist. They will often talk to a journalist, however, if we are agreeable personalities who don't just ask questions but actually listen to the answers, and who seem as intent on understanding the 'why' as we are in getting a headline."

Treating others with compassion and empathy is not just a tactic for seasoned journalists. In fact, it's the surest route to a happy, successful life.

We've shown you the many ways that being a nice person will get you what you want. How a small compliment or gift can lead to amazing opportunities. How saying yes can enhance your relationships. How you can help yourself by helping your rivals or competitors. We've now arrived at the most important skill for anyone who wants to harness the power of nice: the ability to put yourself in someone else's place, to put your head on the other guy's shoulders.

According to Daniel Goleman, people who are highly empathetic—that is, people who are able to understand what others are feeling and see things from their perspective—are happier, more popular, and have better love lives. They're also more successful in business. "Empathetic people are superb at recognizing and meeting the needs of clients, customers, or subordinates. They seem approachable, wanting to hear what people have to say. They listen carefully, picking up on what people are truly concerned about, and respond on the mark," Goleman writes in *Primal Leadership*.

Look at the success of Gordon Bethune, who, as the CEO for eleven years at Continental Airlines, transformed it into what is arguably the most successful traditional carrier in the country. Someone once asked Bethune how he understood people so well. "I used to be one," he quipped. Before Bethune became the CEO in 1994, Continental's rate of on-time arrivals was consistently rated as the lowest in the country—and it was often dead last. Late arrivals were costing the airline $5 million a month. Bethune realized that the best way to motivate his employees to improve service was to make them feel like they were part of Continental's success. So he began a program that paid *every single employee*—gate agents, flight attendants, baggage handlers—a $65 bonus each month that the airline finished in the top five in on-time performance. With 40,000 employees, the program was expensive—$2.5 million a month—but not nearly as costly as being late. By Bethune's calculations, he could improve service while cutting costs.

It worked. Just three months after the program was launched, Continental finished No. 1 in on-time performance for the first time in its history, and consistently made it to the top five. The program did so well that Continental was able to raise the bar. Today, Continental must finish in the top three for staffers to receive the bonus. But they also get a bigger reward—$100—when Continental finishes first.

In the medical profession, empathy is now considered so important that it is part of the required curriculum at accredited U.S. medical schools.[1] Researchers discovered that doctors who show sensitivity to their patients' feelings see fewer lawsuits than physicians who simply offer up cold, dispassionate diagnoses. In his book *Blink: The Power of Thinking Without Thinking,* author Malcolm Gladwell details a study in which medical researcher Wendy Levinson observed a group of doctors. Half of the physicians had never been sued; the other half had been taken to court at the least twice. Levinson found that the doctors who hadn't been sued spoke to their patients for an average of three minutes longer than the ones with litigious patients. They also had softer voices and used humor more. "People just don't sue doctors they like," medical malpractice lawyer Alice Burkin told Gladwell. "In all the years I've been in this business, I've never had a potential client walk in and say, 'I really like this doctor and I feel terrible about doing it, but I want to sue him.'"

Of course, empathy is best learned as early in life as possible. That's why primary schools are now getting in on the act. In Canada, a grade-school program called Roots of Empathy teaches compassion to nearly 40,000 children a year. And in late 2005, the United Kingdom launched a plan to teach emotional skills to British schoolchildren.

One of the key ways that schools teach empathy is through volunteer work. In *The Healing Power of Doing Good,* author Allan Luks describes a program for Texas teens who were in danger of dropping out of school. After the at-risk kids began tutoring at the local elementary school, their dropout rate went from an expected 35 percent to 6 percent.

Helping others not only builds self-respect but can actually improve your health. A study conducted in 2003 at the University of Michigan followed 423 elderly couples for five years. It found that people who cared for others—either through volunteer work or simply by being attentive neighbors and spouses—had *a 60 percent lower rate of premature death* than those who didn't reach out.

HARNESSING THE POWER OF EMPATHY

All of us, barring the occasional narcissist and sociopath, are naturally empathetic. That's why if your mother calls you extremely stressed out about an upcoming holiday dinner, you start to feel anxious, too. It's why you may start to feel sleepy while watching a coworker yawn. Newborns will begin to cry when they hear another baby wailing. "We're exquisitely attuned to the stream of emotional signals coming from other people's faces and postures, and we resonate with expressions of our own. Actual people get under our skin in a way that an abstract problem never will," primatologist Frans de Waal writes in *Our Inner Ape.*

Unfortunately, many of us have lost touch with our empathetic nature. With the frenetic pace of twenty-first-century life—twenty-four-hour newscrawls, the constant barrage of interruptions from cell phones and BlackBerrys—it's easy to become so distracted and overwhelmed that we fail to see the people right in front of us. So here are some ways to reconnect with that lovely ancient DNA that's been lying dormant in all of us:

WHISTLE WHILE YOU WORK

A few years after we started The Kaplan Thaler Group, we bid for the Coldwell Banker account. We really didn't think we'd win it. After all, there were some very big agencies going after this business—all with resources and credentials much greater than ours.

We did a big creative presentation, and we were very proud of the work. But we were still very surprised when we were awarded the business. When we asked the Coldwell Banker execs how we beat out such formidable competition, they told us that of course they liked our work, but they were also impressed by the way we were always laughing and cracking jokes with each other. We really seemed to like each other, they said. The comment surprised us. Granted, we knew that not everyone is lucky enough to genuinely enjoy their colleagues, as we did. But we figured most professionals could get it together and at least *pretend* that they could stand each other when meeting a potential client.

Not true, the Coldwell Banker folks told us, explaining that in many of their meetings they got the sense that the agency people had either never worked with one another or were busy jockeying for position. The Coldwell Banker executives were worried that they'd have to spend more time dealing with the other agencies' internal politics than on building a good campaign.

There is a great myth about the workplace—that if you're having a good time at the office, then you must be goofing off. But Daniel Goleman argues that happy employees are better for the bottom line. Not only are they more productive, but cheerful employees also make customers happy—and happy customers buy more. One study actually quantified the effect that employee morale has on sales, revealing that revenue increases 2 percent for every 1 percent improvement in the service atmosphere.

Goleman found that bosses with empathetic styles—who knew how to listen to their employees' concerns and address them effectively—are better able to communicate with and inspire their workers. They retain their employees longer, and those employees work harder. In fact, a Gallup organization poll of 2 million employees at 700 American companies found that productivity is directly related to their relationship with their immediate supervisor.

Being a likable boss doesn't necessarily mean offering big bonuses, fancy lunches, and Ping-Pong tables—though we're sure our staff would inform us that perks like these are most welcome. Instead, it means respecting the work of every single person in the company. Every job at The Kaplan Thaler Group is important. That's why whenever someone at Kaplan Thaler has a success—be it bagging a $40 million account or selling a fifteen-second TV spot—we always try to acknowledge it. It doesn't matter how small the business is—because for a junior-level person who just sold a coupon ad, that's their whole world. If we don't recognize it, we're essentially saying that their work doesn't matter.

GET OUT OF YOUR MOVIE

Recently, we read about a prank that one frustrated business traveler pulled on a loud cell-phone user. Jonathan Yarmis was in an airline's Red Carpet Club in New York's LaGuardia Airport when he—and everyone else in the room—had to endure the constant jabbering of a man leaving numerous voice-mail messages. The young blabbermouth ignored the many people who asked him to keep his voice down. Since the man had repeatedly broadcast both his phone number and his destination city of Nashville many times, Yarmis jotted down the number. When he got home to Seattle, Yarmis called the talker at 2 A.M. Nashville time.

"I said, 'You must think it's pretty rude getting a phone call at 2 A.M.,'" Yarmis told the *New York Times*. "He said, 'Yeah.' I said, 'It's certainly less rude than the behavior you exhibited in the Red Carpet Club this afternoon.' We both hung up. I made the point to him.'"

Although we don't agree with Yarmis's tactics, he definitely drove the point home. Rudeness is at an all-time high. An Associated Press poll released in October 2005 found that 70 percent of Americans believe we are ruder than we were twenty years ago, citing loud cell-phone users, parking-space stealers, and people who use foul language in public as the biggest offenders.

Most of the folks committing these infractions aren't bad people—they're just clueless. They're so used to their kids' screams and shouts that they don't realize in a restaurant that the little darlings are ruining everyone else's meals. They're so comfortable in their casual clothes that they don't think twice about wearing sweatpants and flip-flops to the theater. It certainly never occurs to them that they're offending the performers with their attire. It's as if everyone is starring in their own movie—*The Bill Show, The Heather Show*—forgetting that everyone else has their own movie, too.

That's why it's important to imagine how life looks from someone else's point of view. Linda's daughter, Emily, recently offered a good lesson in this:

Emily had a few friends over, and I scolded her in front of them—saying she had to do her homework before socializing. Later, Emily said, "How do you think it makes me feel when you yell at me in front of my friends?" Suddenly, I realized how embarrassing that must be. I know how I would feel if someone was criticizing me in front of a client. I also realized that I'd do a much better job motivating Emily to do her homework if I asked her with respect—and in private.

In other words, there were two movies going on: The Linda movie was about Linda being a responsible parent. The Emily movie was about Emily being treated like an adult.

At work, learning to see other people's movies is particularly helpful in creative meetings. For example, if someone presents a pitch idea that we don't like, simply dismissing it out of hand will make the other person feel bad. In addition, sometimes there's a good idea hidden in that pitch, but the person just can't express it. By asking questions like "How did you arrive at that concept?" or "Why did you think it would work for this campaign?" we can often uncover some really terrific ideas.

LISTEN FOR THE FEELING WORDS

When we started working on the Aflac campaign, the insurance company gave us stacks and stacks of information about their company. But we didn't know where to go with it until we met the CEO, Daniel Amos. In the meeting, we were once again given a rundown of dry facts and figures.

So we asked, off the cuff, "What really bothers you the most?"

Amos said, "I'm just sick and tired of going to lunches where nobody can pronounce the name of my company."

That's when the lightbulb went off for us. His family had spent their lives building this company. He had thousands of employees coming to the office every day, and he wanted them to feel proud to be there.

Once he started speaking from his emotions, we could have thrown all those statistics and profit reports out the window. *He just wants people to remember the name of the company.*

And so, under the brilliant creative direction of Tom Amico and Eric David, the Aflac duck was hatched—and overnight became one of America's most well-known advertising campaigns. Since the commercial started airing in 2000, the Aflac duck has become a cultural icon, and in the first few years alone the company's sales went up 55 percent. The Aflac duck has a higher "Q score" (a syndicated research ratio that measures the likability of famous people and characters) than the Energizer Bunny or Ronald McDonald. He has made Aflac a household name, much to the delight of Dan Amos—and the chagrin of Ben Affleck!

ACCEPT INFLUENCE

Dr. John Gottman—the University of Washington researcher with the phenomenally high track record of predicting marital success—says that one of the keys to a successful relationship is being able to accept influence. For example, say you call your husband to tell him you have to work late (as we confess to doing on too many occasions) and your husband says that he's upset because you've worked late every night this week and he was looking forward to having dinner with you. You could just snap at him and say, "Well, do you think I actually *want* to spend the evening scrutinizing invoices?" Or you could be a bit nicer and say, "Sorry, sweetie, but these invoices are due tomorrow."

Or you could consider his point. Because what he's really saying, along with the fact that he feels neglected, is that your marriage should be as important to you as your career. Would the company really fall to pieces if you didn't file the invoices tonight? Is it worth the price—namely, your husband's feelings?

Accepting influence doesn't mean always doing the other person's bidding. Sometimes you have a deadline and you just have to hope your spouse understands. But you'll have a much easier time getting him or her to understand if you have consistently shown that you are considering your spouse's point of view—and are willing to make the necessary changes and compromises.

SEE YOURSELF IN THEIR EYES

"I spent the first half of my life trying not to embarrass my mother and the second half trying not to embarrass my wife," cracks Jay Leno. Jay has never done a wife joke on *The Tonight Show* because he knows that all humor is rooted in truth. "Every comic that you see doing wife jokes—except for the ones that are having a baby or something like that—there is usually something else going on," he says. Leno needs to get laughs to stay in business, but a joke at his wife's expense just isn't funny.

Many of us get so caught up in our own desires and ambitions that we lose sight of how our own agenda might affect others. As bosses, we often forget that the people who work for us often see us differently than we see ourselves. Once, Robin made an off-the-cuff joke to our receptionist after hearing that her assistant had called to say she'd be late because her very old dog had to go to the vet:

"It's always the dog!" I said jokingly. I've had many dogs in my life and was expressing commiseration with the problem: Ain't it the truth—those lovable mutts just take over our lives.

But that's not how our receptionist heard it. She was hearing that the president of the company was angry with her assistant. So she did the right thing: She told my assistant that I was upset. Later, my assistant came into my office, very distraught. She explained that she lived alone and didn't have anyone to help her with the dog. I said, "What are you talking about?" She told me that she'd heard I was mad that she was late. I said, "Nothing could be further from the truth!"

Everyone had good intentions—we were all just in different movies. That's why it's so important to give people the benefit of the doubt. Just because your coworker was curt in the elevator doesn't mean he's angry with you. It could mean a lot of things—that he had a fight with his girlfriend, that his mom went to the hospital again, that it's Monday. When you learn to see the other guy's perspective, you almost always realize *it's not about you.*

When you start practicing empathy, you develop the instincts you need to get out of your own bubble and become more attuned to the needs of others. This will benefit you on both a practical and a personal level. For example, blogger Paul English was frustrated with his own attempts to reach a human being when he called phone and utility companies. So he created a Web site that helps people get out of voice-mail hell, with a published list of the number sequences you need to get a live operator for dozens of companies. He figured that if endless voice-mail loops were making him batty, then there probably were many others who felt the same way. The site was a huge hit and got an incredible amount of media attention, receiving nods on the *Today* show, CNN, *ABC News,* and in the *Wall Street Journal.*

Often, when you practice the power of empathy, the benefits come indirectly—and sometimes years later. Take our friend Erin, an actress who has appeared in many of the commercials we produce.

Erin had the typical New York artist's problem. To get work, you have to live in the city. But living in the Big Apple is prohibitively expensive. Erin knew that when the time came to have a child, she and her husband would probably have to move to less expensive pastures, which would severely hinder her acting career.

But in the meantime, she adored her life in the city, since it not only enabled her to have her dream job but also gave her the opportunity to pursue meaningful volunteer work at a local animal-rescue organization. Erin's task was to pair up the potential adopters with the available dogs, and the rule was that applicants were put on a list and granted dogs in the order that they were requested. "One day I heard from a woman who had just lost her beloved dog after fourteen years of friendship. She was looking for a beagle to replace the one she had just lost," says Erin.

Erin's heart went out to the woman—after all, it was her love of dogs that made her volunteer in the first place. The problem was that the organization had only two beagles available for adoption and a long list of people interested in beagles. "But there was something in this woman's voice that convinced me she needed a pet in her life," says Erin.

So Erin bumped the woman up on the list. " I would later find out that she lived alone, had lost her son and her husband to cancer, and really considered her dog family. This woman's life had meaning with a dog in it, and I sensed somehow that I needed to complete her home with a lucky rescue from our charity," says Erin.

Fast-forward two years: Erin was pregnant and hoping to find a New York apartment that would accommodate her new family and enable Erin to continue her acting career. "We needed a new home with space for a baby, and were having a tough time finding a suitable place. Our friend happened to call with another beagle update, and I shared our good news about the pregnancy and our bad news about our housing crisis. She told me she'd call right back," says Erin. Moments later, the phone rang—a real estate agent, a friend of the lady with the beagle, who had the inside scoop on a fabulous and affordable Manhattan apartment that was not yet listed on the market. Today Erin and her husband have a beautiful little girl and a lovely apartment to raise her in. And her acting career is flourishing!

Whether or not empathy makes you a million dollars or lands you a prime piece of real estate, we believe that turning your attention to others is simply a richer way to live your life. What's the alternative? Obsessing about yourself—your hair, your weight, your finances? The beauty of focusing on other people's concerns is that it shifts your attention away from your own worries and anxieties. And it's a lot cheaper than therapy!

NICE CUBE

NICE CUBE: IRRITATION IS THE MOTHER OF INVENTION

Put a small notebook and pen in your pocket today, and keep it with you at all times. Then watch and listen to the things that people complain about: The photocopier has a paper jam. Someone's neighbor plays their music too loud. The mail carrier always jams letters into the box. At the end of the day, list ten solutions that could solve their problems. By focusing on the needs of others rather than yourself, you might find that you come up with some really creative and innovative ideas.

NICE CUBE

NICE CUBE: STAR IN SOMEONE ELSE'S MOVIE

Think of someone you're having a conflict with. Then write out their perspective on the situation, either on paper or on a computer. The important thing is not to let your hand (or hands) stop moving. Keep the flow going so that you don't overthink the situation. You want to *feel* their emotions, not think them. It's a great exercise to see things from the other person's point of view.

NICE CUBE

NICE CUBE: FIND THE FEELING

The next time you are in a large meeting or on the phone with a friend or relative, make a list of all the feeling words you hear. "I wish"; "I hope"; "I'm upset": What do these words tell you about the person(s) you're talking to? What clues do they give you about how you can better address their needs?

Chapter 10

Create a Nicer Universe

In 1960, a successful French businessman, Marcel Bleustein-Blanchet, created a foundation designed to help deserving young men and women launch their careers. One year, the foundation awarded a grant to a young astronomer, who purchased his first telescope with the money.

More than thirty years later, the astronomer discovered a new planet and chose to name his new discovery "Planet Bleustein," after his very first benefactor. Imagine the delight of the Bleustein family, knowing that their grandfather's generosity was being acknowledged light-years away.

When we began writing this book, we too had no idea just how potent the power of nice was. We knew that being polite and considerate had been important in our business and our personal relationships. But until we began talking with others about the impact that kindness had had on their lives, we didn't realize just how powerful a thoughtful gesture or supportive remark could be. We were amazed by the sometimes long-reaching consequences of seemingly small encounters—helping a stranger with a bag, giving career advice to a young employee. In fact, very often the people *telling* the stories were astonished: Before relaying the tale, they themselves hadn't realized that their success or good fortune could be traced back to a simple, compassionate gesture. After all, they hadn't extended the kindness to land a contract or win over a colleague. They were "just being nice." So they were amazed to see the domino effect of just one thoughtful action.

As we wrote this book, we began to notice a subtle change in our own lives as well. While we think of ourselves as nice people, we certainly can be as thoughtless as the next guy. But as we put down some of our thoughts and insights about the power of nice on paper, we began to act differently ourselves. We were more thoughtful in our day-to-day actions. We took a fresh look at the million little moral dilemmas we all encounter each day. How much should I tip the waiter? Do I give a dollar to the homeless person I pass on the street? Do I cut through traffic on the road or on the sidewalk, or let others have the right of way?

When disagreeing with a coworker, we found ourselves stepping back and trying to see their "movie." If a friend snapped at us, we assumed goodwill first, before reacting with anger. In each conflict we faced, we asked ourselves, "Is there a nicer way?"

And it worked! As a result of writing this book, we have had fewer fights with friends, experienced more compassion for and from colleagues, have laughed more often, and enjoyed even more business and personal successes. We find that we are more sensitive to the effect of a biting remark, more aware of how an unkind word can deflate the creativity and enthusiasm of others—and of the entire organization. And, conversely, we've seen how praise and support can mobilize our entire company to work more collaboratively.

Since we started our company, we have been fortunate to have attracted not only brilliant and talented professionals but some of the nicest people in the industry. And they have formed, by their deeds and actions, a culture where their behavior has been mirrored and adopted by new hires, clients, and the vendors we employ. They have, in essence, created a nicer universe for themselves.

Of course, there is more to success than just being nice—hard work, intelligence, and talent are essential, too. We aren't claiming that being nice is the *only* way to get ahead. Everyone can point to instances where the ruthless jerk got the job, the recognition, the girl.

But we hope that we've been able to convince you that there is another way, that being kind and considerate is an equally valid—and we believe far more effective—way to get ahead than being selfish or cutthroat. So given that, why not take the nice route? Not only will it take you further in your career and in your life, but you'll feel better about yourself. In today's culture, we hear a lot about self-esteem and are offered many ways to attain it—from repeating prayerful affirmations to buying a new car. And yet we frequently neglect the surest and quickest route to self-respect—*behaving in a way that makes you respect yourself.* If you act with integrity, compassion, and class, you might not need to spend hours on a therapist's couch blabbing about how your conflicts with your boss or husband stem from something your mother said when you were four. You will know, in your core, that you are a valuable and worthwhile person who can help change the world, one nice action at a time.

It's a lesson our friend and coworker Hal Friedman discovered not long ago. During his daily commute home from New York City to New Jersey, Hal always saw the same panhandler begging for change near the entrance of the Lincoln Tunnel. "Over the course of several months, he came up to my car every day and I always gave him a quarter or a dollar, whatever I had handy. Over time we got to recognize each other, and the exchange went from a bothersome distraction to a nice part of my ride home," says Hal.

One day, Hal was astounded to see that his friend was wearing a new suit and tie. The man was walking from car to car, smiling and shaking everyone's hand. When he finally reached Hal's car, he proudly explained that he had finally found a job and wanted to thank Hal for helping to keep him going. "Seeing his success and the light in his face was worth a hundred times more than the money I'd given him," says Hal.

If you take anything away from this book, we hope it's the realization that there is untapped potential in even the smallest good deed, and that it can have a multiplier effect strong enough to change the world. Yes, a random act of kindness *can* help you become wealthier, healthier, and wiser. But, most of all, it will make you happier.

And, after all, isn't that the *real* power of nice?

Notes

Chapter 1: The Power of Nice

1. Tim Sanders, *The Likeability Factor: How to Boost Your L-Factor & Achieve Your Life's Dreams* (New York: Crown, 2005), p. 31.
2. Daniel Goleman, Richard Boyatzis, and Annie McKee, *Primal Leadership: Realizing the Power of Emotional Intelligence* (Boston: Harvard Business School Press, 2002), p. 15.

Chapter 3: Bake a Bigger Pie

1. Tom Rath and Donald O. Clifton, Ph.D., *How Full Is Your Bucket? Positive Strategies for Work and Life* (Princeton, NJ: Gallup Press, 2004), p. 31.
2. Survey of about 1 million workers in more than 330 companies conducted by the Hay Group, a human resource and organizational behavior consulting firm, as reported in the *Kansas City Star*, July 11, 2001.

Chapter 4: Sweeten the Deal

1. David G. Myers, Ph.D., "Feeling Good About Fredrickson's Positive Emotions," *Prevention and Treatment*, March 7, 2000. Ruut Veenhoven, Ph.D., "The Utility of Happiness," *Social Indicators Research*, 1988.

2. "The Science of Chocolate." BBC, November 17, 2004.
3. David G. Myers, Ph.D., "Feeling Good About Fredrickson's Positive Emotions."

Chapter 5: Help Your Enemies

1. Robert Axelrod, *The Evolution of Cooperation* (New York: Basic Books, 1985), pp. 7–18.
2. *Washington Post,* July 22, 2005.
3. *Wall Street Journal,* January 3, 2006.

Chapter 6: Tell the Truth

1. Dwight D. Eisenhower, *Crusade in Europe* (Baltimore, MD: The Johns Hopkins University Press, 1997), p. 389.
2. Robin Marantz Henig, "Looking for the Lie," *New York Times Magazine,* Febuary 5, 2006.

Chapter 7: "Yes" Your Way to the Top

1. Tom Rath and Donald O. Clifton, Ph.D., *How Full Is Your Bucket? Positive Strategies in Work and Life* (Princeton, NJ: Gallup Press, 2004), pp. 55–57.
2. Warren Bennis and Patricia Ward Beiderman, *Organizing Genius: The Secrets of Creative Collaboration* (New York: Perseus Books Group, 1998), p. 209.
3. Alan Pease, *Signals: How to Use Body Language for Power, Success and Love* (New York: Bantam Books, 1984), p. 6.
4. Richard W. Malott, *Elementary Principles of Behavior* (New York: Appleton-Century-Crofts, 1971), pp. 4.6–4.11.

Chapter 9: Put Your Head on Their Shoulders

1. "The Infinite Mind," National Public Radio, November 23, 2005.

Index

Aflac, 7, 51, 109
Allen, Woody, 63
Allies
  making, before they can become enemies, 51–52
  treating today's adversaries like tomorrow's, 49–51
Ambrose, Stephen, 58
Amico, Tom, 109
Amos, Daniel, 7, 109
Anger, 66, 68, 69
Arnold, Susan, 97–98
Auletta, Ken, 100–101
Automatic kind gestures, 10–11

Bailey, Brent, 22
Baskin, Elizabeth, 60–61
Beatles, 22
Bethune, Gordon, 102–3
Bigger pie, baking a, 16–28
Bleustein-Blanchet, Marcel, 116
Blink: The Power of Thinking Without Thinking (Gladwell), 4, 103
Bloomberg, Michael, 86
Body language, 30
  detecting dishonesty, 63–64
  mirroring, 34–35, 81
  nodding, 80–81
  open, 54
  peace, gestures of, 53–54
  tilting your head, 54, 81
Boundaries, setting your, 72–73
Breast Cancer Research Foundation (BCRF), 21
Budd, Zola, 47–48
Buffett, Warren, 31, 87
Burkin, Alice, 103

Canada, Roots of Empathy program in, 103–4
Chouinard, Yvon, 24
Clinton, Bill, 51
Clinton, Hillary, 48
Coldwell Banker, 105–6
Competitiveness, 2–3
  complimenting the competitors, 48–49
  helping your enemies, 41–56
Compliments, 30, 37–38, 78
  for competitors, 48–49

Conflict resolution, honesty and, 69–71
Conspiracy of Fools (Eichenwald), 59
Continental Airlines, 50, 102–3
Cooperation, 20–23
helping your enemies, 41–56
Creativity, humor and, 33
Csikszentmihalyi, Mihaly, 24

Darling, Millie, 8–9
Darwin, Charles, 3, 81
David, Eric, 109
Davidovsky, Mario, 87–88
Davis, Richard, 1–2
Decker, Mary, 47–48
Dell, Michael, 86
de Waal, Frans, 104
Dipankara, Atisha, 25
Doctors, empathetic, 103

eBay feedback form, 45
EchoStar Communications, 36–37
Eichenwald, Kurt, 59
Eisenhower, Dwight D., 57–58
Ekman, Paul, 64
Electrical Products of India, 32–33
E-mails, responding to, 85–86
Emotional Intelligence (Goleman), 91
Emotions, expressing, 60–62
Empathy, 100–115
Enemies, helping your, 41–56
English, Paul, 112
Enron, 59–60
Ergen, Charlie, 36–37
Ethical Brain, The (Gazzaniga), 58
Experts, advice from, 65

Firing an employee, 87
Fischer, David Hackett, 49–50
Five-Finger Discount (Stapinski), 33–34
Flattery, 30, 37–38
Ford, Henry, 80
Foxwoods, 92
Framing the debate, 52–53
Friedman, Hal, 119
Friends, 43–44
Fry, Art, 23

Gallup polls, 106
Gazzaniga, Michael S., 58
Gestures. *See* Body language
Gifts, small, 36–37
Gilbert and Sullivan, 22
Gingrich, Newt, 48
Gladwell, Malcolm, 4, 103
Goleman, Daniel, 4, 30, 33, 64, 102, 106
Good Business: Leadership, Flow, and the Making of Meaning (Csikszentmihalyi), 24
Gottman, Dr. John, 77, 110

Hamwi, Ernest, 19–20
Hassini, Tony, 16–17
Healing Power of Doing Good, The (Luks), 104
Heen, Sheila, 70
Henning, Doug, 16–17
Heublein Distillers, 93
Honesty. *See* Truth, telling the
How to Talk to Anyone, Anytime, Anywhere (King), 62
Humor, 32–34, 78

Imitation, 34–35
Influence, ability to accept, 110
Instincts, listening to your, 64–65
Internet, career opportunities and, 18
Ipsos-ASI, 52
IQ, 91
Ireland, Kathy, 18–19

Jackson, Judge Thomas Penfield, 100

Karnett, Diane, 8–9
Karp, Ruth Downing, 93–94
Kerr, Michael, 33
King, Larry, 62
Kipper, David, 68
Koval, Robin, 11–12, 35, 45–47, 84–85, 87, 93, 111

Lafley, A. G., 21–22
Laughter, 32–34
Laybourne, Geraldine, 36–37
Leno, Jay, 24, 53, 91, 96, 110–11
Leo Burnett, 50
Levinson, Wendy, 103
Lévy, Maurice, 70–71
Lincoln, Abraham, 37, 97
Lincoln on Leadership (Phillips), 97
Listening
  being quiet and, 90–99
  to the truth, 59–60
Lukeman, Gerry, 52
Luks, Allan, 104

"Management by Wandering Around," 97
Marital success, predicting, 77, 110
Mentoring, 20
Miller, Shira, 20
Mirroring, 34–35, 81
Multiplier effect, 6, 119
Myers, David G., 29

Negative impressions, 11–12
Nestlé, Henri, 22
Nice Girls Don't Get the Corner Office (Frankel), 3
Nonverbal communication. *See* Body language; Tone of voice
"No," saying
  effects of, 78, 82
  ways of saying "yes" instead of, 84–88

Opportunities, expanding, 16–18
Optimism, benefits of, 79–80
Origins of Virtue, The (Ridley), 23
Otto, Charlotte, 21
Our Inner Ape (de Waal), 104
Oxygen network, 36–37

Pai, Lou, 59
Parker, Chan, 8–9
Patagonia, 24
Peace, gestures of, 53–54
Pease, Allan, 80–81
Performance, winning based on your own, 45–47
Pessimism, 80
Peter, Daniel, 22
Peters, Tom, 97
Pharmavite, 22
Phillips, Donald T., 97
Pillsbury, Whitney, 32
Pine, Rachel, 29
Pooling of resources, 20–23
Positive, staying, 76–89
Positive impressions, multiplier effect of, 6–7, 119
Post-its, 22–23
Primal Leadership (Goleman), 4, 30, 102
Principles, Power of Nice, 6–15
  negative impressions are like germs, 11–12
  nice must be automatic, 10–11
  people change, 9–10
  positive impressions are like seeds, 6–7
  you never know, 8–9
  you will know, 12–14
"Prisoner's Dilemma, The," 44
Procter & Gamble, 21–22, 97–98
Productivity
  employee-supervisor relationship and, 106
  humor and, 33
  positive feelings and, 30, 78, 106
Publicis Groupe, 70

Republican Party, 52–53
Revenge, resisting impulse for, 42
Ridley, Matt, 23
Roberts, Kevin, 50
Robinson, Dr. Ona, 73, 79
Rudeness, 107–8

Saatchi, 50
Sacks, Oliver, 64
Samsung, 48–49
Seligman, Martin, 79–80
Serling, Rod, 52
Sharing, 23–24
  of credit for an idea, 25–26
Signals (Pease), 81
Silver, Dr. Spence, 22–23
Skilling, Jeff, 59
Smiling, 34–36, 78
Social intelligence, 91

Sony, 48–49
Stack, Fritz, 35–36
Stapinski, Helene, 33–34
Stout, Martha, 63
Supreme Commander: The War Years of Dwight D. Eisenhower, The (Ambrose), 58
Survival of the fittest, myth of, 2–3
Susan G. Komen Breast Cancer Foundation, 21
Sweetening the deal, 29–40

Telephone calls, responding to, 85–86
Thaler, Linda Kaplan, 10, 35, 54–55, 65–66, 72, 87–88, 108
Thank-you notes, 85
3M, 23
Three Tenors, 49
Tone of voice, 30, 63
Truman, Harry, 25
Trump, Melania and Donald, 7
Truth, telling the, 54–55, 57–75
  boundaries, your right to set, 72–73
  difficult news, personally delivering, 66–67
  finding strength in the weakness, 68–69
  helping others find the truth themselves, 67–68
  positive truths, starting with, 65–67
  resolving conflicts, 69–71
Twilight Zone, The, 52

University of Michigan, 4, 104
U.S. Bank, 1–2, 50
U.S. Department of Labor, 25

Valdez, Lupe, 76–77
Vampire bats, 23
Veenhoven, Rutt, 29
Volunteer work, 26–27, 104

Wall Street Journal, 86
Washington, George, 49–50
Washington's Crossing (Fischer), 49–50
Waterman, Robert, 97
Wauton, Chris, 92
Weaknesses, finding strengths in the, 68–69
Weis, Charlie, 88

Yale University School of Management, 35
Yarmis, Jonathan, 107
"Yes" your way to the top, 76–89
  ways to say "yes" instead of "no," 84–88